# THE ROAD
## TO DUTCH HARBOR

## JOE ALASKA

iUniverse, Inc.
Bloomington

iUniverse books may be ordered through booksellers or by contacting:

iUniverse
1663 Liberty Drive
Bloomington, IN 47403
www.iuniverse.com
1-800-Authors (1-800-288-4677)

ISBN: 978-1-4502-9183-5 (sc)
ISBN: 978-1-4502-9184-2 (e)

Printed in the United States of America

iUniverse rev. date: 3/1/2013

TO MY MOTHER

# TABLE OF CONTENTS

# INTRODUCTION

I consider myself a simple guy.

Toys and possessions do not mean a lot to me. But there are exceptions. There are ALWAYS exceptions. I would rather enjoy unique experiences. For example, travel to new and different places. Unfortunately there is no limit to this. I have tried to keep it practical and realistic. So I combined my love of America with my love for road travel. This has resulted in me seeing a LOT of the USA. I really enjoy taking the back roads. Especially remote roads. The less traveled the better. Until I get bored with that, it will continue. While I have been to Mexico and Canada a couple times, I strongly prefer the USA.

One of my favorite pastimes is playing golf. I am not that good, which is sad considering how many rounds I have played. So I combine the driving with the golfing and take a golfing road trip whenever I can do so. I try not to make any firm plans. It is fun to be flexible and let the trip just happen. I always have a great time, and usually have no idea where I will golf next until I stumble on a course.

New experiences for me also include living in different areas. Widely different. I loved my home town, but I never thought I would live there all my life. Some people may not understand that. Not putting down roots? Just not for me. Maybe I am more like a tumbleweed. Stopping every once and awhile, but eventually breaking free to move on. Tumbleweeds can spend a lot of time jammed up against fences. Like being in the paint business for 16 years. But eventually they break free. THANK GOD!

Where do I begin? Well, I was born in Wadsworth, Ohio. I spent a few early years in nearby Rittman. It was all fond memories. Warm summers and running barefoot in the grass. When my family moved to Naperville, Illinois, it was just a stepping stone. Next we moved to Louisville, Kentucky. I was entering the 4th grade and my whole life was ahead of me. I remained in Louisville for almost 20 years. Loved it. But I knew there were other places to experience and enjoy. To this day I follow the Louisville Cardinals and Kentucky Wildcats. I may have been born in Ohio but I consider Kentucky my home.

I graduated college with a degree in Business Management. Up until then I had worked various jobs. Way back, I started making money sweeping floors at a local dry cleaner in Naperville, Illinois. During high school I was a busboy at one of the best restaurants in Louisville. Later I was a clerk in a big produce department. There was a stint in a county grass cutting crew maintaining the roads. I also worked at my dad's place, a company that made printing cylinders. Related to that, I worked on a high speed printing press, mainly producing cigarette cartons. Then I was an usher at major rock concerts, back when there was specific seating.

For a few months I worked at a large company that made Moon Pies. I dusted off pipes in rooms where there were huge sifting machines mixing up flour and sugar. It was hot and sweaty, and I left the job each day feeling like a big cookie.

They suddenly moved me to tarring a new roof. It was a great job working with a view of all the action at the main airport in Louisville, Standiford Field.

Then I spent one of my favorite summers working as a cowboy at a dude ranch in Colorado. Near Estes Park.

When I graduated from college I concentrated on positions in sales and management. I tried selling business forms. Turns out I hated selling, and was not very good at it.

So I took a job running paint stores. At first it was retail, but I soon moved into commercial locations. I took a transfer from Louisville to Fremont, California near San Francisco. Then to a bigger branch in nearby Emeryville, CA. It was a bad situation at that branch, and eventually I went to a competitor who moved me to Phoenix, AZ. This was during the housing boom in Phoenix and we sold LOTS of paint to big contractors painting all of those houses.

Changes were made after a few years, and my position was eliminated. I left with a nice severance package and was eligible for rehire. I played golf for a few months, and kept in touch with upper management. I loved Arizona and The Sonoran Desert. But the next thing I knew they offered me another store in Dayton, Ohio. I had gone to college there at The University of Dayton. So I went back there for a few years, also working in a new store in Centerville a few miles outside of Dayton.

But I wanted to get back to the West, specifically Arizona. It was at this time I met my buddy Dean who was a salesman at my branch. He also wanted to GO WEST. He got out first, moving to Albuquerque to work with a painting contractor. About a year later I was moved to Garland, Texas near Dallas. It was not Arizona, but I was getting closer.

As soon as I arrived in Texas there were problems. I had been transferred there to run the commercial branch in downtown Dallas. But that was now changed. I was put in a small retail store in Richardson, which was scheduled to be closed in a year or so. But I was told there was a new location being built in which I would be moved. OK. Well, just before Christmas a year later my boss and his boss walked in with some news. My store was now being closed, and the other location would not be built.

So once again I was given a very nice severance package. Two packages from the same company, not bad! Most unusual.

Now I thought I should take my time and look for a job I would really like. I wanted nothing to do with the paint business. I tried to get into Golf Course Management, but everyone wanted me to start at the very bottom at very low money. So I played a lot of golf for a year as I learned this was not the dream to pursue. When my money in the bank reached a certain point, I packed up and moved myself to Phoenix where I would lower my goals and just make some money.

The first summer I was a courier driving around the metro Phoenix area in a car with no air conditioning. Then I was an assistant manager at PetSmart for awhile, then assistant manager at a big swimming pool company. AGAIN I tried sales, selling Lazy Boy furniture, then vacuum cleaners (for one day), and finally I even sold viaticals. (Look it up.) Meanwhile, I had gotten a real estate license and sold homes at the same time I was doing some of these other jobs.

But the bottom line was I needed more money. And I finally reached the point where I bit the bullet and made the phone call I thought I would never make. I called the paint company again, same one that let me go twice.

Looking back, I wonder which one of us was dumber?

The paint business was booming, and there was interest in hiring managers. They hired me and started me in the Scottsdale branch. Shortly I was moved to a downtown Phoenix branch. Things went very well. It was very hard to make bonuses, yet I was making them quarterly and annually. Out of 500 branches in the USA mine was in the top 25 in all the good stats. I hung in there for 3 years or so, but I just was not happy. I never was happy since I returned. So I heard of a job opportunity with a new company. They actually were one of our customers. It was a manufactured home company that bought their paint from us.

And I took the leap. I quit and left a salaried position to go back into sales one more time.

Maybe it was a bad decision. Maybe I did it just to see the expression on the face of my boss, who I hated, when I gave my notice. Leaving the company was good for me, but that new job just did not work out as expected. But it was still good for me.

It all came to a head in a perfect personal financial storm about two years later. The money was not as expected at the new job, so I just quit. And now the housing crisis was just beginning. My adjustable rate loan which had not changed for 5 years suddenly was ballooning. Each month it was going up, and pretty significantly. My house was suddenly unaffordable. I had to sell and get out of that loan. I had no job and no job prospects. And I had to move somewhere. Hard to decide WHERE with no job.

THIS is where the story actually begins.

Good thing I was single. Happily so. I am somewhat of a loner, and very independent. That is how I was able to move all around the country, play all that golf, and do all of that road cruising I mentioned before. There would be no pressure except from myself, and that was enough.

But, first things first. There is NO road to Dutch Harbor. You would need to eventually put your car on a ferry, as you are going to an island. Unalaska Island.

Eventually I ended up taking the drive of a lifetime. Phoenix to Fairbanks via The Alaska Highway. This was an indirect route to Dutch Harbor, but I was not going to Dutch at the time.

But I am getting ahead of myself…

# TIME FOR A CHANGE

Like I told you, I sold real estate for six years. And I knew the housing market was collapsing. Especially in Phoenix. The comparable sales supported me pricing my home at $200,000 . Seven years earlier I had bought it for $104,000. I put it up for sale at $195,000. And I was willing to negotiate. At the same time I hit the internet. Using CareerBuilder, I started looking for a job. If I had to sell my house, I wanted to make a change and move to somewhere different. I searched for a job in Nevada, Utah, Idaho, Wyoming, Montana, Alaska, and occasionally Colorado. I wanted to avoid populous states, so Colorado was borderline. That also meant I was looking in states with fewer opportunities.

And I listed my home with a realtor. My license was long expired. Plus, I did not want to mess with it, as I had other stuff to work on. So I called an old friend where I used to work, Anita. By the time the deal was over, she was still old, but no longer a friend. She put the listing on the MLS where other realtors would see it. This is common with realtors, and it often works. But that was all I got, so I could have used anyone with the same result. In the end she actually cost me money. So in the future, I will NEVER use a realtor. I think the internet will kill off this PROFESSION soon.

I loved my house, but would buyers feel the same way? It was the typical Arizona mauve stucco. Gravel front yard, pretty basic. The selling point

1

was the back yard and view. As soon as you enter the front door, you see the view out the back. The Sierra Estrella Mountains in the distance and a huge cotton field in front. There are no houses to interrupt the scene. But there were rumors of a development taking over that cotton field, with houses and commercial zoning. It would ruin my view. THAT was the reason I was OK with a move. Now that I have moved away, that project has been put on hold due to the depressed market.

My backyard itself was also a selling point. It was small and fenced. But it was an eclectic garden with many varieties of cactus and desert plants, as well as citrus trees. I planted anything that could grow, then I formed narrow paths that wound through it all. Often late at night I took a stroll out there. In the dark, it was outright hazardous, as there were cacti in all directions a few inches off to either side.

My house was in general good shape. The biggest issue was the air conditioning which would need replacing. It was working, but was on its last leg. Also, a pipe leading to the backyard sprinklers was leaking. Then there was some cavitating of the backyard soil. It mainly was an issue when I watered the garden. The owner before me had put in some nice planting soil when he started that garden. He put that dirt in a large part of the yard. It was very soft, and did not compact very well. When I watered heavily, occasionally the earth would open up as a mini-sinkhole. The water would drain into that hole and go who knows where? Part of the problem was burrowing animals, so the water had easy places to flow. There were ground squirrels as well as toads. I would refill the sinkhole with dirt as best as I could. But the same thing would happen somewhere else.

I spent many evenings with my patio door wide open. There was the time I had a large toad in my living room. I did not notice him until I looked up from the newspaper I was reading. He jumped into the working part of a reclining chair and it got interesting trying to find him.

That was the worst of it. It was a nice house.

I got an offer in a few days. FULL PRICE. A young single girl. She did her 10 day inspection and it all went well. BUT, just as her 10 days were ending she pulled out. It was her right. Even for STUPID, NONSENSICAL REASONS. She had gone to the internet and found out there were registered sex offenders in the area. Well DUH. They are everywhere. ANYONE can enter their address on that internet site and the map points out all sex offenders living nearby. There are no exempt areas. In many states, if you get arrested urinating in public, you are labeled a sex offender. GOOD LUCK trying to find a home with none of them nearby.

So, I put the home back on the market. And that market was getting worse day-by-day. I reduced the price to keep it attractive. It was a smaller model home in a neighborhood of bigger houses. SO, it was the cheapest home in the neighborhood. And it showed well. A retired couple, who had looked at the home when it first went up for sale, came back again when they saw it back on the market and reduced. I just wanted an offer.

They made one. It was pretty low. I now had the house at $179,000. They offered $155,000. But they indicated that they would have the house inspected, but would accept it as is, or not at all. In other words I would not be asked to spend more money on repairs. I accepted the offer.

The second offer came ten days after the first offer fell through. That ten days cost me $40,000.

Just when the second deal was about to close, something happened with the buyers loan. They got an interest rate a bit higher than expected. It was a problem, and they were about ready to walk. I ended up buying it down with my own money. The buyers were calling my realtor and got no answer. She was out of town just as my deal was falling apart. So I negotiated with them myself. $5000 more out of my pocket. But it was a good decision. The housing market was in big trouble. That same house is now worth only 75 or 80 thousand. I still made enough money to pay off my debt and finance my move.

OH YEAH, just as my house was being sold I got a job offer. Finally I had a break.

I had been doing a daily search of job opportunities on the internet. By searching daily, I was able to only look at the newest listings. I responded to anything close to being interesting. Early on I decided to tell everyone right up front that I would pay for my own move, unless their policy allowed for that. Otherwise, many employers would eliminate me immediately and search their local area.

There was the distinct possibility I would sell my house before I had a job, then what? I put a lot of thought into it, and chose Reno as a default location. I had been through there several times, and I liked the landscape. Close to the mountains and wide open spaces. It was a growing city, still not huge. Many job opportunities.

I even talked to a realtor there about home prices and rental opportunities.

There were a few nibbles for employment, and three options came up which seemed to be the best.

WINNEMUCCA, Nevada. A medium sized town in the northern part of the state. I had been through there before, even stayed a night. My impression was of a quiet town. There was one golf course. A new company was building a plant there to manufacture trailers. I would be a shipping / receiving manager. Good money. The bad news was there was very little available apartments or homes in the city. Nearby gold mines were booming and they had hired many new people who filled up all the vacancies. I had an initial phone interview which went very well. But it petered out after that. Later I went through the area again and I got a bad second impression of the town. Glad it did not work out.

GILLETTE, Wyoming. Interesting job. I would assemble last minute crews needed to clean up train derailments. It would be a position where I was on call 24/7. When the phone rang, it was GO TIME. I would be based in Gillette, but would serve a five state area. That all appealed to me. It would mean living at the wreck site until it was cleaned up. Once again I had a phone interview that went well. The guy I talked to ALSO had a background in the paint business, so we connected. He wanted to meet me, but was not wanting to pay for my trip. I said I would pay to fly to Gillette for a weekend. I interviewed again face to face. It felt good. But he told me he had another good candidate. I drove around town later looking at homes and apartments. I felt I would be moving there soon. Another medium sized town, and it even had 2 golf courses.

But again, they hired the other guy.

Then there was ANAKTUVUK PASS, Alaska. Never heard of it. A population of 350 or so. Mostly Inland Eskimos. When I saw the ad I had to read it several times. I felt like I was not qualified, but it just said they wanted a business degree and management experience. I would be General Manager in a Native American Corporation that ran the hotel, general store, satellite TV operation, restaurant, and fuel depot in a small community in the Alaskan Bush. Only accessible by air. 150 miles north of the Arctic Circle. I would report to a Board of Directors. The pay would be good, and they would give me a house to live in. They would also pay for my move up there.

When moving to Alaska from the lower 48, it is rare for employers to pay for your move up. It usually is a free move for someone who will not stay long at the job.

I sent a long letter with my resume, basically saying I was someone who was qualified. Then I was blunt, thinking it was all or nothing. I told them I was crazy enough to LIKE the chance of living there. It was soon obvious that they were having trouble finding candidates. A few weeks later I heard from them, a complete surprise. I was in the running, and they wanted to run a background check.

Next I got a call from the company lawyer, who lived in Anchorage. He wanted to set up a time for a phone interview with him and the Board President, Larry.

The interview lasted almost 2 hours. They asked a LOT of questions. Some questions I had no good answer, like WHAT DO YOU KNOW ABOUT RUNNING A FUEL DEPOT? I was honest. If I did not have the right answer, I told them that. My selling point was that I was a MANAGER. I managed people. The guy who manned the fuel depot NOW knew what to do, and I would learn from him. Plus, I knew I was a good candidate, and I knew they were desperate.

The lawyer, Dave, asked most of the questions. Larry was pretty quiet. I had a mental impression that he was a small older man. Turned out he was 32.

Next thing I knew they were calling me and making an offer! A real shock. I had never been to Alaska, but had always wanted to go. AND I now knew where Anaktuvuk was. WAY NORTH. Somewhere I would never have seen otherwise. I had heard of The Brooks Range, now I would be living there. I never heard of Gates of The Arctic National Park. Now I would be living in it. It was a HUGE national park. I did as much research as possible on the internet, but it still did not really set the stage.

At the time my house deal was in escrow, so accepting the job was all contingent on the deal closing. If it blew up, we would have to all sit down and figure it out. That is why I was motivated to just get it closed, no matter what. I appreciated them working with me on that.

Now I had to worry about the big move north. I could have flown up and had all my stuff shipped right behind me. The company would have paid for it. But I wanted to drive. I wanted to see The Alaska Highway. The final leg of the trip, north from Fairbanks, would be on a nine passenger plane. So I decided to travel light. I looked around and realized I owned a bunch of CRAP. There was no real value in it except to fill a house. The house I was given in Anaktuvuk was furnished and stocked with all the basics. I did not have a lot of stuff. I just need the basics. So I decided to sell or give away what was of value, and throw out the rest.

The selling never happened. I planned on a yard sale, but I did not have the time and I did not want to mess with it.

The final week I put up a sign that said FREE STUFF. All of a sudden I was finally meeting all my neighbors. A Mexican guy pulled up in a pickup truck and took a bunch of furniture. He also took a lot of record albums. I kept some of the very best, but not ALL of It He took away David Bowie, Gentle Giant, and Yes. I am sure he took it only because it was free. Kids in the neighborhood came by, then came back again. I gave one of them a full stereo system. EVERYTHING MUST GO!

Now I was committed to leaving on Monday. My deal on the house was also scheduled to close on Monday. I had seen many real estate deals blow up at the last minute. It was crunch time. The title company would be able to direct deposit my proceeds into the bank.

The buyers of the house said I could leave stuff that they may want. That helped. I left a couple beds and some basic furniture. Also garden tools, hoses, etc. They could throw it out if they wanted. I stayed up late the last night finishing cleaning and packing. It was a huge job, and I did it all myself. The last thing I did was unhook an old floor model TV and roll it out to the end of the driveway. It had been a gift from my best friend Dean in New Mexico. I kept it blaring as I packed, cleaned, and moved out. It was on until the last minute as background noise.

Monday was also trash pickup day.

That TV was set by the curb around 1 AM. Next morning I was up at 6AM, and it was already gone. The neighbors had made one last scavenging run. The only things left were some real odds and ends.

My neighbors were very efficient. I hope they are still enjoying that stuff.

For the last few days I had been packing the Toyota. Strategically and scientifically. I needed to use every inch of space. And I did. When I shut that door for the last time, it would barely close. It would hold everything I owned, including two cats and myself.

That takes me to YELLAFELLA. He was a very friendly, and vocal, neighborhood cat. I had FOUR of my own when I first moved into that house. The day I moved in is easy to remember. The same day as the 9-11 attacks. When I let the cats out to their new home, it took them all of 15 minutes for them to find out how to get on the roof.

Yellafella became a regular visitor to the house. He ate the food I set out for my cats, and he hung around with the gang. He was not there everyday, but most. I realized he was a NEIGHBORHOOD cat at some point, owned by nobody but fed by many. I decided to take him with me on the move. At that time I had only one cat remaining of the original four. The other three were planted in my garden all holding spots of respect. FLUFFER was the last one left. She was a kitten I took in as part of a real estate deal a few years prior. The sellers told me they were moving and were taking all of their cats, except one. Sure, it sounds like a scam. They told me they were turning in the last kitten to the animal shelter. I took the bait. And I took that last kitten, FLUFFER.

The rest is history.

On that final weekend I was waiting for YELLAFELLA to make his usual appearance. If he did not SHOW, he would not GO. As usual, he came by. Lucky for him.

I wanted to continue my tradition of adopting a cat the day I was moving. The same situation happened a few years earlier when I moved to Arizona from California.

So when Yellafella made an appearance, I locked him inside the garage. I did not want him leaving via the cat door the night before I left. He was not used to being locked indoors. I had him and Fluffer in the garage overnight until the last minute. Then I loaded them. I put Fluff in a cat carrier that had stuff piled on top. I knew she would stay in there until I dragged her out. Yellafella was different. I never had him in a car. Who knew what to expect? I put him in on top of all the crap, and he immediately tunneled through to the back window. As I sat in the driver seat I could only see out the front and sides, the entire back end was packed. At first there was a lot of crying and yowling, then the cats did the same thing. But soon we all calmed down.

When I backed out my driveway the car bottomed out as I went down the curb. The Toyota was grossly overloaded. I drove slowly as I left. It was the first house I had ever owned and I loved it. But I only remember bits of us leaving. We headed out east on Lower Buckeye Road, and hung a left on Estrella Parkway northbound.

I would be heading north for the next week, and more.

# DRIVING TO ALASKA

We got on I-10, then 101 north. Leaving the metro area, we caught I-17 heading toward Flagstaff and I settled back. It was a long way to FAIRBANKS, ALASKA.

The first day we were heading to Kanab, Utah. My sister Fran and her boyfriend lived there. I was dropping off half of my carload of crap for storage there. This was the personal stuff I wanted to keep, only valuable to me. And Fran was going to take Yellafella. She wanted a cat and Yellafella wanted someone to take care of him. It was a great match. That would give FLUFF and me a little breathing room for the next week of driving. Until I got to Kanab I could barely move. We would spend the night in Kanab. The first day of driving would be relatively short and easy. The next day the real driving would begin.

After Kanab, I would go into CRUISE MODE. With the excitement of the trip, I would be up everyday at daybreak. Then I would drive until dark and stay wherever I was at the time. REPEAT, until I was in Fairbanks.

So Phoenix was in my rear view mirrors and we were leaving The Valley of the Sun. The drive was uneventful except for one last chance to ogle the scenery. First I left the saguaros of The Sonoran Desert and climbed the Mogollon Rim. We passed Bumblebee and Cortez and went through the high desert near Prescott. We climbed to 7000 feet into the pines of Flagstaff. Just for a few miles we were on I-40, then north on 89 into Indian country. The pines disappeared and I was now in the red rocks. North through Page, a great little town in northern Arizona. I was able to look at the golf course there as I drove by. Page National. It had been my pleasure to play it a couple times in the past. Then we left Arizona as we crossed The Colorado River at Lake Powell. We cut across southern Utah just north of The Grand Canyon. An hour later we were in Kanab.

Fran was waiting for us when we arrived. Yellafella quickly adapted to his new home. And Fran adapted to her new cat.

We all had a nice dinner at their house. There wasn't a lot of room at Fran's house, so I stayed down the street in a semi-famous hotel, The Roberts Inn. It has been visited by MANY old time movie stars, and the pictures on the walls prove it. Their rooms have names. Fluff and I stayed in The James Arness room. Fluff preferred staying under the Arness Bed. We had breakfast there next morning, along with 80 German tourists who cut ahead of us after getting off their bus.

After breakfast, I said goodbye to Fran and her boyfriend Mike. The evening before, we had unloaded much of what was packed in the car and put it in local storage. There was still a lot left. It filled up the trunk and a good part of the back seat. Now Fluff and I were ready to cruise.

Fluff was sleeping in the back as we left town on RT 89, choosing to hunker down in the cat-carrier. The door was open, but she wanted to stay inside for security. That cat made most of the trip in that carrier.

Soon we were in Long Valley. I turned left on a small road that went over the ridge toward Cedar City, RT 14. It would be a rare chance to take one last back road before I was living BEYOND all roads. Then we hit I-15 and headed north. We would stay on that road until it ended at the Canadian border. The Utah countryside opened up ahead of us. There was a definite sense of exhilaration, I was finally on my way. I set the cruise control at the speed limit and relaxed. Soon I saw the first snow covered mountain in the distance. It would be the first of MANY as we headed north for the next week.

As I drove near Richfield there was evidence of a bad range fire that had come through the area the year before. It had blackened most of the ground, but not everything. I remember hearing how fast it moved, and it was difficult to slow the fire down and put it out.

The first big city we would go through was Salt Lake City. I had been through there several times and had positive impressions. Nice modern city by the mountains. This time I would have a different opinion, even though I was just passing through.

It was time for lunch. I rarely take a sit down lunch while traveling. So as I entered the metro area I pulled off at an exit that appeared to have a lot of commercialization. There was a sign that said a Burger King was to the right, and I made the turn. Now I was on a stretch of road that had warehouses for about a mile. When I looked ahead and saw more of the same, I turned around and headed back to the interstate and headed back north. I went a few more exits and pulled off again. After I drove a short distance, there was a sandwich shop. FINE. I pulled in and listened to the guy ahead of me place an order. It sounded a bit complicated, where they basically wanted you to tell them each ingredient you wanted. You have it built the way you wanted. Too many ingredients, though. It was probably good once you tried it a couple times. I ordered roast beef on a bun, but it was not that easy. The questions just kept coming.

Finally, after a frustrating couple of minutes, it was done. I pulled up behind that other customer ahead of me. I could hear the discussion, and it was not good. Turns out he is ALSO confused about the ordering system, and is not getting what he thought. So the sandwich had to be REBUILT. After a few more minutes, I pulled around and left. It was now a half hour of screwing around.

Maybe I SHOULD hit a sit down place!

I drove back to the interstate and headed north for ten more minutes. One more time I saw a sign. Again, it was Burger King. I pulled off, made the turn, and went up a long hill to a light. As I sat there I could see down the road ahead and I saw no Burger King. Surely if I kept driving there would eventually be a Burger King. But I wanted FAST FOOD. I made a U-turn and got back on the interstate for good.

Was this one big inside joke the locals played on travelers? Were there ANY Burger Kings?

I made up my mind I would not pull off until I could see a restaurant. Actually SEE it. Meanwhile, the traffic was very heavy. Everyone was flying. And the interstate was having construction done, just to keep it interesting. I left the city and metro area more hungry than ever.

Next thing I saw was a rest area, so I pulled over to give Fluff a chance to go to the bathroom. I had a leash to keep her secure. So I drove to the far end where it was semi-quiet, and took her out for a walk. She was petrified and only wanted to hide. Earlier in the day I had tried the same thing near Long Valley. Same result. I had other cats that were similar. They got in a car and shut down all bodily functions until the end of the day when the driving stopped. So this is what we did from then on. There would be a cat box in the hotel room. She knew to take care of business then, or wait. It seemed to work out the rest of the way.

I was happy to be out of Salt Lake City. After just a few miles more, I saw a restaurant. Ironically, it was a Burger King. I grabbed some food and ate as I drove on.

The scenery seemed to improve as I headed into Idaho. Vast vistas with mountains in the distance. I hit Pocatello during rush hour, and I kept going. Then I checked out the map and did some estimating. It seemed I would be getting near Montana as it was getting dark. I prefer to pull over at that time and find a motel for the night. Driving at night indicates some sort of HURRY. There were a few small towns just before the border, so I would pull over at the first place I saw. Well, these were very small towns, and they had no motel. So I headed on into the dusk.

I saw a town about 50 miles ahead on the map that seemed bigger, and more likely to have facilities. So I resolved myself to one last stretch of driving at the end of an already long day. Then I came around a bend and saw a sign for LIMA, and there was a hotel right there. GREAT.

There was a mini-mart as well as a restaurant. Only one other car in the parking lot. It was probably owned by the guy working behind the desk.

The room was cheap.

Lima, Montana. Had never heard of it until I slept there.

The man working in the lobby seemed genuinely interested in my travel plans. He told me what was available in Lima, which did not take long. The main point was to go across the street to the local restaurant. He said it was good food. There was another place to eat, where you cook your own food on a big grill. I was not in the mood to cook, but to be waited on and relax.

After registering I went to the room. I did not ask if they allowed pets, so I discreetly carried Fluff in from the car in the cat carrier. I let her out and she immediately did her ritualistic panic run to under the bed. She would cower there awhile while I brought in what else I needed, which was not much. The room was nice. Quaint. Small town touches and eclectic furniture. The bathroom was a little rough, but OK. Hey, it was one night. I had a little whisky, so I watched a bit of TV and had a couple of shots. Then I headed across the road to the restaurant, LENA'S.

The place was about half full. I sat down and grabbed a newspaper. The friendly waitress took my order, then I relaxed and soaked up the local color.

I saw an article in the paper about crossing the border into Canada. It told of long waits to clear customs, but the long waits it described were north of Seattle, WA. I would be crossing north of SHELBY, Montana.

ANYTHING involving police and governments makes me nervous. I had looked up information on the internet about crossing the border into Canada. Most of the concern was regarding taking a pet across, and what was needed. Shots, vaccines, that type of thing. Before I left Phoenix I got all the required documentation, at a cost of about $100. Fluff got the shots.

But that article got me thinking about what lay ahead. Tomorrow afternoon sometime, I would be at the mercy of some Canadian. Possibly Royal, possibly Mounted. Or a nasty combination of the two. What could happen? So I enjoyed my meal. I caught parts of conversations as I sat there. Some people were traveling like myself. There were also locals. My guess was they were farmers of some sort, probably from BIG farms. After all, it was MONTANA. BIG parcels of land, maintained by BIG machines. It is one of my favorite states. Always big mountains in the distance. There was a nice mountain just outside of town.

I took my time at dinner and left a nice tip. Then back to the motel. Fluff was still under the bed quivering, but came out in a few minutes.

Shortly I heard some noise outside, someone else taking a room next to mine. At one point I went outside to get something out of my car and my new neighbor was sitting outside his room. He was having a beer and enjoying the view of that snow-capped mountain just to the west. I HAD to strike up a conversation. He was a semi-local, working in the area. He would take a 20 mile dirt road to work each day, to a mine. We hit it off right away. I ended up giving him a few hats from my PAINT DAYS in Arizona. I used those hats for golfing. But I would not be golfing a lot where I was going. For some reason I had packed a box of new hats, even though space was at a premium. The hats were left over from trade shows where we gave them out to contractors. Now they would be DEAD WEIGHT when I flew to Anaktuvuk Pass. Eventually I told my new friend I had to hit the sack. I had a last shot of whiskey. It had been a good day. I would leave as soon as I woke up in the morning. As usual.

It was around 7 AM when I left. As usual, the last thing I loaded was Fluff in the carrier. Discreetly. She traveled well. Usually she would find a hole to hide in, like behind the seat on the floor. She was too fat to get underneath. Most often, she just stayed in the cat carrier with the door open. She went into a semi-trance state of sleep.

There were still only a couple cars in the parking lot when I left. First thing I did was turn away from the interstate and pull into the GAS N' GO for a fill-up and my typical breakfast, a large coffee. It was a beautiful morning and I was in the middle of God's country. It would only get better. 100 miles to Butte.

It was a Wednesday morning and not much of a rush hour. Very few cars. There would only be one decent-sized town before Butte, and that was Dillon. It was about halfway between Lima and Butte. I stopped at a rest stop with a great view of the Pioneer Mountains to the west. Big Sky Country says it very well.

It took an hour and a half to get to Butte. It is an old town built around a huge pit mine. As you head north out of town and climb into more mountains toward Elk Park Pass, you get a great view of it. The Berkeley Pit Mine. As I descended from the pass, I noticed a general rule of interstate highways being broken. There were several 45 MPH curves. It was simply a matter of letting Mother Nature win a battle but not the war. The engineers routed an interstate through steep mountains and deep valleys. They gave in and followed the curves of the land, and the routing of a river. The movement of dirt was kept at a minimum, allowing the scenery to remain natural. Oh, and it is a lot cheaper. This is typical in many mountain states, especially Colorado. But I do not recall any 45 MPH zones on I-70 which crosses that state. And it goes through Glenwood Canyon.

Generally, interstates move ANY dirt needed to keep the speed limit UP. And they choose a routing that allows that. I drove onward to Helena, the state capital. A beautiful setting. A town in a valley with mountains all around. Then I made a gradual climb into what I call high desert. The trees disappear and there are wide open grass ranges with rolling hills. I get a bit euphoric in these settings. Travel in the USA is what I love, and THESE areas are what make it COOL. Until I see all there is to see in the USA, I have little motivation going to other countries. There IS motivation, just not as much.

Maybe a bit under 100 miles to Great Falls. As I got within 30 miles or so I caught a glimpse of some huge wind turbines sitting on a high ridge to the west. They were huge, but hard to tell HOW big, as there was nothing around to give a scale. I lost sight of them as I dropped down into the valley where the town lay. But I again caught sight of them in my rear view mirror. There was a lot of road construction going on, and maybe that is why I did not have the greatest impression of Great Falls. Sorry.

As I left town for the final dash to Canada, I started another big climb. The hills were even bigger than before. Up and down, on a grand scale. Rolling hills. Down for a mile or two, then back up for a mile or two. Huge farms on both sides of the highway. Not sure of the crops, but it looked massive in scale. Not a lot of people on the road.

Then I reached SHELBY. A relatively small town in northern Montana most red-blooded Americans probably have never heard of. But it is at the intersection of I-15 and Route 2. I-15 is a great interstate, but it kinda goes to nowhere. OH, eventually you can get to Calgary and Edmonton, but you need to be motivated. That is what I was doing, and maybe that was the goal. But I think the same rough goal could have been accomplished a bit differently. Right now, it is the best way to go to ALASKA. Through Montana. You would think it would be north from Seattle. No sir.

I had been through Shelby a year earlier, hanging a left on Route 2 to head towards Glacier National Park. A must see for all Americans. Route 2 used to be the MAIN east-west highway for the far north US, before the interstates. I still plan on taking it on a future trip, beginning to end. Just to do it. TODAY, I just stopped for a final fill up of USA gas and a quick gas station snack. Shelby is not a beautiful town by itself, it is OK. But it is in the middle of awesome terrain. It feels remote.

Once again, as I head north I climb. Now I really get the feeling of solitude. I am in the middle of nowhere. Just me and the farmers who live all around me, but I see none of them. Stark. It is roughly 40 miles to the border. My cat had all her papers, and I had zero contraband in the car. But I was nervous about the border crossing. It was a new world after 9-11. I had crossed that same border several times before, and it was nothing. But that was years ago.

As I approached the border I saw a couple of SLOW moving planes flying along the border, about the size of a single passenger Cessna. In this area there are farm roads which cross the border or are right by the border with no official security. The locals are the ones who know where they cross. Or maybe a terrorist. I proceeded and finally came over a hill where I saw the border ahead. There was one car ahead of me. So much for those big lines.

I pulled up behind the other car. Someone told me through a loudspeaker to back up to a waiting spot where they could view both the front and rear of my car via cameras. FINE. Eventually it was my turn. I pulled up. The guy at the window asked for my ID. I gave him my drivers license, and he kept it.

Then came the inquisition. What are you doing in Canada? Where are you heading? How long will you be in Canada? How much money are you carrying? Are you trying to smuggle a cat across the border? OK, I was kidding about the last one. But, as soon as he heard I was heading for Alaska and I was an American, he said to pull in and see THE GUY inside.

The cat thing never came up. Fluff chuckled. Someone needs to update the internet.

I parked and went inside. There was a girl in front of me at the counter. As I listened she was stressing out. She was coming to Canada to live with her boyfriend. The BAD thing was she was coming to Canada looking for work. Turns out Canada had a bunch of unemployed folk already. They did not want another person, especially an American, joining the unemployed pool and competing for those jobs. Not sure how it ended, but it did not sound good.

Meanwhile, Royal Canadian Officer Bob opened a new line to personally hassle me.

They had kept my license and now BOB had it. He had already run a check on his DEEP BLUE supercomputer. And he already had the results. DAMN THE INTERNET!! He then asked me if I had any major crimes on my record? I only had one official one, which I told him about. There was a DUI in Phoenix a few years ago.

It was embarrassing to talk about it, but he asked. I know it was a mistake. Big mistake. He asked, I answered.

Now, Mr. Royal Canadian Not-Mounted-At-The-Time Policeman was ready to take me down.

I did NOT mention that 32 years ago I was arrested for possession of one joint of weed. I went to court and they ended up dismissing the charge. The judge told me my record would be expunged. EXPUNGED. He specifically told me I could say it officially NEVER happened. The judge was evidently wrong.

So OFFICER BOB saw the record of that charge, and asked why I did not admit to it. I told him it was supposedly expunged. He laughed and said I had a bad lawyer. But he liked that I did tell him what I THOUGHT was correct, and that I was honest with him. He did the cop thing and said he COULD arrest me, that he COULD put me in jail. But NO, he would not. He would give me a break. This was an option I think they offer to 95% of the people in my same situation.

See, they can give you a temporary permit to pass through the country. Of course, there is a fee.

PAY MONEY, and its all cool.

And they accept American dollars. And credit cards. ANYTHING.

They made me stand in another line to pay for my permit / fine / bribe. It was around $200. I just wanted out of there. It was obvious I HAD to drive through Canada to get to my new job in Alaska. And I had always wanted to drive The Alaskan Highway, most of which is in Canada. But I have no motivation to return. Canada is just an extension of the northern USA. If you include Alaska, any beautiful scenery you can see in Canada can also be seen in the USA. So why would I go through the hassle again? Eh?

AND, I would certainly hope we give the same treatment to those Canadians coming south through our border.

# CANADA, GATEWAY TO ALASKA

Eventually they cut me free. I went out to the car and Fluff was still asleep and unaware of the near crisis. As I pulled out I was paranoid about being pulled over, but I got over it.

I had been to Canada before, several times. Now my impression just across the border was boring and dreary. I already missed the USA.

As I went through Milk River I noticed a GOLF COURSE sign. The first of MANY in Canada. While I now hated at least one aspect of Canada, I respected the MANY golf courses I passed en route to Alaska. In EVERY town I entered, I immediately looked for a golf course sign, and THERE IT WAS. IMMEDIATELY. Just before the various liquor stores.

I headed into Lethbridge. I saw a few signs referring to the university there. The University of Lethbridge. U of L. It hit home as I am a long time University of Louisville fan. The real U of L. The better U of L.

The road through town curved as it followed the lay of the land. There were a few deep ravines that cut through town. Eventually the road had to cross that ravine and there was a nice bridge. The sad thing is that bridge was the highlight of Lethbridge. EH?

I had a message on my phone to call the title company about my house sale. As a former realtor, I dreaded what the call was about. I assumed the deal had blown up at the last minute. I needed the cash to make the move to Alaska. Sure, I would be reimbursed from the company. But I was cash poor at the time. I pulled over and listened to the message. It was good. My deal had closed. As I sat by the road, I transferred the funds to a credit card. The stress was gone and I was solvent. As a former realtor, let me tell you, if you have a general common sense you do not need a realtor. BUT, if the whole process confuses you, THEN you need a realtor. Most people do NOT.

So I left the greater Lethbridge metro area, heading west to Route 2. I turned north toward Calgary. It was an exciting straight and flat stretch of road. Maybe exciting to the locals. I turned on local radio and heard the weather forecast of ZERO for that night. Sounded a bit colder than I expected. Eventually it hit me they were talking CELSIUS. Zero degrees C =32 degrees in the real world of Fahrenheit.

I headed STRAIGHT north to Calgary, where I figured to get a room for the night. But I got there during rush hour and got caught in the flow. I did not see any signs for lodging, so I drove on. On the north side of town I saw some motels. I pulled over and tried to find a room. After a couple of tries, and finding no rooms available, I jumped back on the freeway and headed into the dusk. It was becoming a large unpopulated area.

Surely small-town Canada could offer shelter. But I looked at the map and knew it may be awhile. Eventually I saw a sign to Carstairs, and lodging. I pulled off and headed west. As soon I headed west I was blinded by the setting sun. After a couple miles I saw a sign for a local golf course. So I knew I was close to town.

When I came to a stop light I guessed LEFT. Jackpot. I found a hotel with a room. There was a number of crews from various companies staying there. And partying on the balcony.

When I checked in I talked with a nice older guy at the desk who told me where everything was in town. Liquor and pizza. I took Fluff into the room, where she panicked and ran under the bed. Surprise! Then I headed out. Liquor and pizza. I enjoy buying pizza from places I have never heard of, the LOCAL pizza places.

I found the liquor store and went in. It was a bunch of bottles stacked on table tops. Looked like it was a restaurant 2 weeks ago. When I tried to pay in American dollars it was a problem. A MINOR problem. The nice lady did not know what to do. I had heard that day on the radio that the US / Canadian exchange rate was EQUAL. US equals Canadian. Historically the US dollar was always higher in value. But the US dollar had dropped in value so badly that it was now equal in value to the Canadian dollar. It was big news on the local TV, as it had just happened.

The nice lady had heard something about THAT, so she took my US dollars. Hey, it was only a pint.

Then I went a block away to get the pizza I ordered. AGAIN with the exchange rate issue, but minor. When the manager was asked to help, he said no problem.

Back to the hotel where I wolfed pizza and watched TV. Fluff came out from under the bed. Canadian TV is interesting. Most of it is the same as the US. BUT, they got the Hockey Channel which is REAL exciting. I think it was pre-season at the time. That night Edmonton and Calgary were playing, a local rivalry. Preseason and it was ALL THE TALK.

WOW. Pre-season hockey. Up until then, I never knew it existed. Yet, I endured.

Tomorrow I would head into virgin territory, beyond Edmonton. Years ago I had driven through Calgary and Edmonton on a big road trip to Banff. On that trip my buddy and I did not even know we were going to Canada until we were in Wyoming. We ended up going 500 miles north of the border, and experienced no shakedown as we crossed into

Canada. We returned east to International Falls before returning to the USA. That was a great trip.

Now I was back. Like having a bad dream again. But even though I was in Canada, I slept well.

Next day I was up at dawn. I packed everything including the cat and headed out.

Today it was getting interesting. I knew I would get past Edmonton, less than 2 hours away. Then I would head west. And the big towns would be behind me. And the smaller towns would become less frequent. Good stuff.

I prefer to travel while it is light. First of all, I enjoy the scenery. Then there is the safety feature of breaking down in the wilderness while it is dark. So I get up when I see light and drive until it is almost dark. I was heading into a region where I may need to pull into a hotel when there is two hours of light left. Because the next hotel is 3 hours away. This issue would increase in importance each day until I reached Fairbanks. Every afternoon I started looking very carefully at where I was on the map and what was ahead. Planning. I wanted to travel quickly, but I would not push things.

I have done a lot of road driving. I knew what I was doing. My new job was waiting whenever I got there. There was no real need to push things. Later I would learn the hurry was all in my mind. I could have taken a few more days and all would have been cool. Wished I knew that. Maybe I would have played some of those golf courses.

But today I had to do some shopping. I needed to buy winter clothes. Lots of them. Suitable for 40 below. Of which I had NONE. From socks and shoes to head wear. And all the naughty bits in between. I had been asking around, including in Carstairs, about where to shop. I heard twice from people that MARK'S in the Edmonton Mall was a good place. Sold.

And I knew there were NO malls after Edmonton, until Fairbanks. The mall in Edmonton is on a list of the biggest malls anywhere. There are around 600 stores there, and I bet a Radio Shack is one of them. Oh yeah, there is a water park there.

So I drove the 2 miles east from Carstairs to Route 2, and hung a left. North to Edmonton, straight as an arrow. Not a lot of excitement in between. Flat farm country. EVENTUALLY Route 2 just peters out and dies in Edmonton. The freeway starts to have traffic lights. I noticed signs to the Edmonton Mall miles before I got there. Obviously a destination for most people coming to town. Kinda sad.

Edmonton was a pretty boring town for me the visitor. Calgary had hills and valleys, much better.

I drove through town and followed the signs. The mall was on the west side of town, where I would exit the area anyway. When I got near it, I wanted to park somewhere safe. I had a car full of everything I owned. And a cat. A lot of it in plain sight, as the trunk was full. THEN I saw signs warning customers that a lot of break-ins had occurred in parking lots there. Management would not be responsible…

Being a Manager, I LOVE that line.

So I circled the whole mess twice, the whole mall, then chose a spot by random luck. I hoped I was near MARK'S. I parked and headed in. I saw a customer and asked where was MARK'S. He told me and it sounded close.

I entered the mall at a secondary entrance. The back door. I passed the food court, walked another minute, and I saw the sign: MARK'S. The mall was huge and I had somehow chosen the right entrance.

When I entered the store I noticed I was possibly the only customer. I headed toward the winter clothes section, which was most of the store. Hey, it WAS Edmonton.

Eventually someone came up and asked if I needed help. It would be their easiest sale of the day. I told them I was moving north of the Arctic Circle, and I had nothing. Grab what I need and take it to the dressing room.

I got it all. Shoes, socks, pants, underwear, shirts, coats, gloves, and hats. A little of everything. Hey, it gets cold there. But I would work in a warm office. I was getting ready for when I went outside for the fun of it. I did not know what to expect. Earlier I learned that the weather extremes were about +90 to -65. Should I be getting a swimming suit? No.

I made it clear up front I was in a hurry. I had a terrified cat waiting. It took 15 to 20 minutes to try on everything. It added up to about $1100. Not bad. Except my credit card raised a flag and the merchant had to call the card company. It took another 10 minutes to get everything straight, but it went through.

When I left I stopped at the Kentucky Fried Chicken in the food court. It could be the last time I saw one for awhile. It was a 3 piece meal and cost about 12 bucks. Welcome to Canada. EH?

I returned to the car with all my new CRAP and made a packed car even more packed. I had trouble finding a place for the food. When I stopped for the night I would re-pack for efficiency. I knew Fluff was in there somewhere, but had no details as to where.

It was the WORST Kentucky Fried Chicken I had ever had up to that point. Very greasy. Maybe they counted that as the gravy. Like I said, very expensive. Maybe they charge extra for the grease.

Just to keep it interesting, I got mixed up on my sense of direction when I left. So I wasted a half hour figuring it out. Eventually I headed west out of town. Finally I was feeling some euphoria about heading into the wilderness. I had no idea where I would spend the night. And, I was loving it.

I was seeing signs for Jasper, Alberta. This was the farthest I had ever been to the northwest until now. But instead of heading south to Jasper, I caught route 43 toward Whitecourt. While it was virgin land for me to travel across, it was uneventful. I hit Grand Prairie at rush hour, and it was pretty slow going through an average sized town. I filled up my gas tank and headed northwest to Dawson Creek. It would be a perfect place to spend the night.

For one thing, it was getting dark. PLUS, it was the official start of THE ALASKAN HIGHWAY. Did you know most of The Alaskan Highway is in Canada? If they called it the Mostly Canadian Highway it would not be as mystical sounding. The hotel I pulled into was a half mile from MILE ZERO of the Highway. In a way, the REAL trip would start next morning.

I ordered a pizza from a local company and watched TV until I fell asleep. Pizza continued to be the bill of fare on this trip. I wanted something quick and tasty. And it gave me a bit of the local flavor.

Next morning I woke up with the sun.

I went across the street and filled up on gas and had my regular large coffee for the road. My first stop was a quarter mile down the road, where I entered The Alaskan Highway. I had wanted to be right HERE for years.

Well, there is a little monument there, at mile ZERO. So I took some pictures. There were many fun facts, like it was almost 1500 miles to the end at Fairbanks. I think they should have put a sign up where I entered Canada at Sweet Grass, Montana that said WELCOME TO CANADA. GATEWAY TO ALASKA.

I headed Northwest. It started out with a whimper, nothing spectacular as far as scenery goes. Some distant hills, that was it. I knew there was a golf course in the community. As a JOKE I had been looking for the right opportunity to just pull over and play a few holes. With a cat in the car. The course was right by the road and I drove by. I saw there was a heavy frost and nobody was playing. If I could not get out on the golf course right away, I was going to keep on driving. This was the case, and I drove on.

It was a relatively short drive to Fort St. John, maybe 70 miles. There was still no sense of wilderness. Houses scattered about. Room to breathe, but that was it. There was a nice bridge crossing the river into town, and a climb in elevation. It was a quick trip through town. No more BIG towns for quite a while. The biggest would be Whitehorse.

Then Fairbanks.

I was now entering an area not covered in any detail on my US Atlas. There was a page featuring a map of British Columbia, but it only featured the southern part. I was in pine trees and rolling hills. Finally I saw mountains ahead. This was getting GOOD. And there were low clouds moving in. I continued to climb up in elevation. Finally I was getting some action. Maybe too much.

Visibility was getting low. And I noticed that, at last, there was not a lot of traffic on the road. Especially heading south. I pulled over just to listen to the silence for a couple minutes.

Snow started to cover the road. I was in no hurry. When I pulled out and drove onward I slowed down from the regular CRUISE MODE. The snow continued to get heavier, and I was still an hour and a half to Fort Nelson. The next BIG town. LOVED IT!

About a half hour from town the road was getting pretty slick. There were no sharp turns, but I took it easy. FINALLY I felt like was in the wilderness and on my own. If you took my picture I would be smiling. Driving The Alaska Highway and snow was moving in! This was what I wanted, a real TASTE of the highway.

When I pulled into Fort Nelson I turned into a gas station. The car needed gas. After I filled it up I went inside to pay. There were a few customers standing around and a nice looking girl manning the cash register. So I asked her about what she knew about the road ahead. TRUBBA. There was a truck that wrecked and blocked the road. Oh, and a snow plow had an accident. Besides that, no real problems.

It was midday, and there was plenty of daylight left. So I was considering driving on. It was a debate. I could drive slow and take it easy. But there was no room for error. Watson Lake was the next real chance for a hotel room. About 300 miles northwest. There were a couple of mom and pop motels on the way, but they were small and easily filled or not open at all. I made a common sense decision and called it a day. It really should have been no debate, but I was in that cruise mode.

Turns out I got lucky and made the right decision.

I got a decent room at a hotel, and took a short ride to see what was in town. Not a lot. Just a few options for food. I hit the local pizza place (as usual) and ordered a pizza for lunch, as well as a sandwich for dinner later on. Then I killed the afternoon in the hotel room as the snow continued to fall. I watched some baseball game on TV.

There was a cable channel there that was like CNN, just the Canadian version. As I was watching I was amused as a story came up about a freak early winter storm centered around Fort Nelson. The only place in Canada with some snow, and I was right in the middle of it.

The snow stopped in late afternoon, but it did its damage. It was a challenge just using the stairs to the second floor to get to my room. Nobody had shoveled them yet. I ate that sandwich for dinner and got a good nights sleep.

Early next morning I got my coffee and headed out of Fort Nelson. The roads were slick and I was amazed at the amount of snow fell that fell the day before. For a short while I second-guessed my decision to stop driving yesterday, as the roads were not real bad. But after a few miles I started climbing the mountains. There was very deep snow where I was now driving. As I went over a mountain pass I had to drive very slowly.

It was obvious that plows had only recently cleared the road but the surface was still icy and slick. I was glad I stopped where I did.

The views were stupendous. I was on THE ALASKAN HIGHWAY. YEAH!

And now there were very few cars coming from the other direction. Love that isolation!

As I drove on I saw a couple of small lodges that may or may not have been open. If I had tried to PLOW forward yesterday I may have had to go all the way to Watson Lake. It would have been epic, but I could have done it.

Like I said, the Canadian TV said it was a local storm that I was caught in. And they were right. After maybe an hour and a half I drove out of the snow. No snow anywhere. Maybe it was the elevation thing, but I was still near mountains. As I drove on it was hard to believe what was just behind me.

I entered Stone Mountain Provincial Park. Beautiful. Mountains here and there as I drove through relative flat land. I came across a herd of buffalo that stretched across the road. Slowly I drove right through them. They were obviously used to seeing people, and just stared back as I passed by.

Soon after that I entered Muncho Lake Provincial Park. Much of the same scenery, and another herd of buffalo. I was getting used to it. They were not afraid of me. I also stumbled across several moose as well as a couple of big horned Dahl Sheep on cliffs I passed. I did not want to mess with them. This was a two lane road that was winding between mountains. Speed limit was about 55 MPH, although it was in kilometers per hour there. EH?

Eventually I popped out of the trees and drove right along Muncho Lake. It was a long lake. How long? Can't say. I had only vague maps of the area. For some reason this part of Canada is cut off from the maps of the provinces. It just does not exist. Except on the map of CANADA, which is hurting on local detail. Obviously I needed to buy a better map.

Along Muncho Lake I was overtaken by a large truck. I think it was a logging truck. So I picked up the pace a bit, but he still was catching me. Finally he turned off somewhere, but this was a rare occurrence of traffic congestion The scenery was beautiful, but was monotonous. I wanted ALASKA.

A HUGE milestone for me was when I came around a curve in the road and saw a large sign. ENTERING YUKON TERRITORY. The Yukon. Up until now it was a place I never expected to see. A place I heard of in cartoons. Now I was there, and I was approaching the town of Watson Lake.

When I got to Watson Lake it was early afternoon. I had a notion to stay there for the night. The next big town was Whitehorse, almost 300 miles away. I pulled into a gas station. After I filled up the tank, I went in to pay. It was a busy time there, as several vehicles had all pulled in at once and now there was a line. As I stood there, I struck up a conversation with a lady behind me.

I asked her if there was any motels before Whitehorse. She told me about a nice place that was relatively unknown, just a spot on the map. The point was there WAS an option to stop somewhere before I got to Whitehorse. I chose to drive on.

Now that I was in THE YUKON it seemed to be a new level of isolation. Nice scenery, but nothing spectacular. Lots of trees that hid the big picture. They were probably just hiding more trees.

It needs to be mentioned that I continued to see signs for local golf courses as I entered any and every town. I wished I had a chance to explore the local golf. When I saw the GOLF sign in Watson Lake I was surprised as I was getting farther north.

As I got near Whitehorse there was a large lake to my left. I drove along it for some time, finally heading west. Then as I was just outside Whitehorse I saw a very nice golf course to my right. I wished I could play. Much later I would realize I could have taken an extra WEEK driving up. The job would still be waiting.

Then I entered the town. A strange town. All around was beautiful scenery, but the town itself was seedy. I drove through it for some time, looking for a decent hotel. It took several rounds. I made an initial goal of finding some food. FINALLY I saw a Quizno's. Hey, a sandwich was all I needed. But it was closed (at 6 PM). I ended up at a Kentucky Fried Chicken, again. The girl at the drive up window was evidently new. It took awhile just to make the order. I ordered a meal, and she asked me if I wanted mashed potatoes. I said yes, knowing that was part of any KFC MEAL in the USA. WRONG. In Canada you get fries. And now I also got potatoes. Then there was the greasy chicken, again. Like it was a gravy. Dripping. Disgusting. And I actually ate some of it. But not all of it.

Next I wanted to buy some bourbon. I had to ask a few people where to go. I found the place, which was discreetly marked. I went in and entered what appeared to be a business office. No booze in sight. A girl came out and asked what she could do for me. BOURBON. She pulls out a menu. A Menu. It had a list of what they had to offer, mainly those little bottles you get on airplanes. I had to ask for a quote on a pint. It was acceptable. We transacted. She went into the back room and eventually came out with a pint. I do not know why they hid the booze from sight.

I paid and got the hell out of there.

Driving around was a risk in itself. I pulled into a food store that was closed, and a beggar came up looking for a handout. I said no, but he ran after me. I saw people urinating by dumpsters. There was a lot of Native Americans on the streets. They seemed to have nowhere to go.

I found the best hotel I could find and went in to register. The lady was behind bulletproof glass, and I signed in. There were several signs saying NO PETS. And more signs saying there would be $250 added to a credit card if they saw a pet. Five minutes later I was smuggling FLUFF into the room. The filthy room. I did not want to walk in bare feet. I ate some of my greasy chicken, but threw most of it away. There was college football on TV as it was a Saturday night. Florida was beating someone.

TEBOW! He was Tebowing before it had a name.

Next morning I just slowed down to get coffee. I could not wait for Whitehorse to be in my rear view mirror. It was good to be hitting the road. This was the HEART of the trip. I was far from civilization in both directions. As I exited Whitehorse there were nice mountains to my left, south. As I headed due west, I went up and down various ridges. At one point I saw a huge bull moose by the road, and I stopped for some pictures.

After I cleared a certain ridge I saw some white on the horizon. My first thought was clouds or fog. Soon I could tell it was snow, on HUGE mountains. Finally I had a great view of a never ending chain of mountains, snow capped. The Nutzotin Mountains, part of The Wrangell Preserve. They extended to the northwest. It was awesome. It went on FOREVER.

And I was almost to Alaska!

It was THE moment of the trip. I was in remote wilderness, and I could actually see Alaska, USA! I was looking at Kluane National Park, as well as Wrangell-Elias National Park. It took a long time to get to those snowcaps, and I enjoyed every moment. The road made a beeline straight to those snowy mountains. Every so often I pull over while on a road trip, just to do it. Just to stop, turn off the car, and get out. It is usually just for a few minutes. I only do this when I am in the middle of nowhere. No traffic going by.

So I took a few pictures and listened to the wind going through the tall pines. Normally at this point I try to imagine what it was like at this exact spot a hundred years ago. Two hundred years ago. What did it look like when the early settlers came through? Most likely just as I was seeing it right now. Less the straight paved road. Then it gets weird to imagine what THOSE folk were thinking when they came through. Possibly the same thoughts? I have to admit I wish I had the experience of seeing this land as one of the first outsiders coming through to settle in a new land. What a battle!

Meanwhile FLUFF had come out of the Back Seat Cave and was yowling at me to get back in the car. So I did. I got back behind the wheel fully relishing the moment.

Set to CRUISE.

Eventually I reached the base of the mountains. Haines Junction. I turned northwest and had a close up view of the mountains as I climbed to new adventures. It was a beautiful Sunday morning with very little traffic. After a couple hours I saw a large lake in the distance, Lake Kluane. The road followed the shore then headed in toward the mountains.

There was road construction and I was stopped at a flagman sight for 20 minutes. Not a bad spot to be stuck. Evidently roads need maintenance even in the most remote areas. But eventually we were waved through, and I continued along the lake. A transition area between mountains. After awhile I hit a bad stretch of highway. The asphalt had buckled, continuously. I figured it was due to earthquakes, but I have also heard about FROST HEAVE. WHATEVER it was, it slowed me down dramatically. A 55-65 mph road was now 35 or less, otherwise I would ruin the shocks.

The last decent-sized Canadian town was Beaver Junction. The scenery seemed to be on hold, and I blame it on Canada. Yes, I may hold a grudge and I may still be bitter. But the best thing about this particular area was that it was leading to awesome Alaska.

I have to admit that after driving through a few hundred miles of tall pines I was looking forward to the open vistas of wide open scenery. Not that the trees were ugly, but they were repetitious and seemed to hide the good stuff just beyond.

After my friendly experience at the US / Canadian Border I was apprehensive about re-entering the USA at Alaska's border. And I was now approaching it quickly.

It was required that I had to drop off my temporary permit at the border before I left the country. I do not know why and I do not care, but that "border" for the Canadians is 3 miles before what the rest of the universe calls a "border." I found it and pulled over. After what happened when I first entered Canada I expected another hassle. It was Sunday morning, and a bit slow I assumed.

Inside the building a nice-looking lady took my paperwork and said, "Thank You, EH?" OK, I lied about the EH. But that was all it took. Not in the mood for chit chat, I hit the road wanting to get back to the USA.

Soon I climbed a long ridge, the first interesting road feature in a while, and the border was right there. A nice AMERICAN guy greeted me. He asked for ID, then he asked me to pop the trunk. I did. There was nothing to hide, but I was nervous. AGAIN I mentioned the cat I had, but he could care less. DAMN THE INTERNET. Then he said, Have A Nice Day.

And I proceeded to do exactly THAT.

# FINALLY. ALASKA!

ALASKA!

Suddenly, I was there.

It was a few minutes down the road before it really hit me. I knew I really arrived. Having driven the USA EXTENSIVELY without ever getting to Alaska, I was long overdue. It was my DREAM ROAD TRIP, and there was still more to come.

At this point Canada was just a bad taste in my mouth, not sure if I will ever return. Of course, that is probably fine with them. FINE being the operative word.

The road led through tall timber. There was Northway, then Tetlin Junction. Onward toward Tok. The Alaskan Range, a huge line of snowy mountains stretched to my left, the southwest. Stretching over the horizon. THIS was Alaska.

Tok is an interesting town. Very small. But it has a big Westin Hotel. Something seen only in bigger towns like Anchorage and Fairbanks. My guess is that it is on The Alaskan Highway and is a natural place to stop, versus driving on to Fairbanks. I stopped in town and got some gas and food.

Tok is also known as the place where it got to minus 73 just a couple years ago. Inland Alaska is unusual where it gets to extremes in temps, both hot and cold. For example, Fairbanks can get to +90 or minus 65. There are not too many places that have that range.

Then I took advantage of being in cell phone range and called home to my family. After that I headed northwest. A long straightaway toward a big mountain range, then the road veers north to Fairbanks. It is an uneventful stretch. I am in pine country, more tall pines. They block any scenery. I may as well be in Florida. There are mountains all around, but I cannot see them. The scenery was very nice, but redundant. As I have said before, I want to see off into the distance. That is why I moved to the southwest and Arizona.

Now finally I was approaching Fairbanks. The first thing you do is go through North Pole. It takes about 2 minutes. It is a suburb of Fairbanks. When you enter the town there is a huge snowman to greet you. Kids all over the world send mail to Santa Claus there, and the post office cooperates. They have staff who respond. It is a big job. There is a big Air Force base there, Eielson. I drove along a runway that goes forever. Across the road was a big US Army base, Fort Wainwright. I guess that is our first line of defense against the Russians. More important a few years go than now.

As soon as you leave the metro area of North Pole, you are in Fairbanks. It is not the city's best first image. Car lots and industrial areas. There was some daylight left, so I took a tour of town. It did not take long as it is not a large town. There are mountains in most directions, but the town itself is relatively flat. I would term the city as a smaller big town. When they built The Alaskan Pipeline, little sleepy Fairbanks had a growth spurt.

It is mainly an east-west town, with several major roads heading that direction. You can get from anywhere to anywhere else in 15 minutes or less. The downtown is small but interesting. Quaint.

Soon I was looking for a hotel. I knew it would be for a few days, so I wanted a place with some entrance besides the front door. On the entire trip I had just avoided the pet policy situation. There was no time to look around after a long day of driving. While some hotels would have allowed pets, I did not even ask. I just snuck her in. When I left, there would be no obvious signs a cat had been there. I made sure of that.

The WESTIN had only one entrance, so I moved on.

Eventually I found the Super 8. They put me in the back, near a rear entrance. It was PERFECT. Then I told them I would need no room service, and everyone was happy.

The next day was a Monday. I wanted to buy some odds and ends from civilization before I headed north. Mainly bedding stuff. I also wanted to look into selling my car. It would not fit in the plane, and there were no roads to where I was headed. Not much of ANYTHING except scenery and solitude. You have to take the good with the bad.

Funny how good and bad varies with the person.

First I called my new boss to check in. He said I could take my time getting organized in Fairbanks. No rush to head north. He also suggested I meet with the company bookkeeper who lived and worked in Fairbanks. Sherrie. So I called her, and we agreed to meet for lunch that day. We went to a local BBQ place right downtown. Really good! She was very nice and was blunt about what I could expect when I arrived. This was a unique position, where there had been a high turnover of previous managers. She was hoping I would not be the next victim. Smart lady. It was like she was testing me to see if I REALLY wanted to be doing this. Almost trying to talk me out of it.

We discussed who I would be working with directly. She told me about the good and bad aspects of working for a Board of Directors. Eight bosses. She told me about The Board President, Larry, who I would eventually consider as my real boss. Finally she told me about the workings of the corporation, and life in a small Alaska Bush village. I had considered all of these things before moving there, but I knew I was qualified and they needed me. I had the Management background, I was single, and I was open to doing something as crazy as this job.

If it did not work out, so be it.

Sherry turned out to be a big help for me in doing my job. She never got the credit she deserved. The best thing for her was she had the real world to escape to when things got frustrating. Me, I would be stuck there, like it or not. I had to maintain a positive attitude. At worse, it was an opportunity to work in a spectacular, isolated location. Inside a huge unknown national park, Gates of the Arctic. 150 miles north of The Arctic Circle in The Brooks Mountain Range. At best I could improve the problems the village was experiencing, and at the same time making a nice living for myself.

Sherry and I finished lunch, then she offered to give me a tour of the city. We saw the historic old section of downtown. She took me by the airport to show me where I would be flying in and out. There was a SPECIAL area for the smaller bush planes, on the OTHER side of the airport. We also went to a spot where you could see the Alaska Pipeline. That was pretty neat. It is four feet in diameter, and was elevated above ground at that location. The construction of the pipeline back in the 70's brought a huge boom for Fairbanks. The line went through town, but the city was also a staging area for material and equipment heading north on the haul road, The Dalton Highway. ICE ROAD TRUCKER fans know what I am talking about.

Sherry dropped me off at my car, and I went to take care of some errands.

First I went to the local SEARS and bought some new pillows and covers. I wanted to sleep on a clean bed. I got a few clothes items, and I was done.

Next I hit Alaska PARK AND SELL, as I wanted to sell my car. I considered storing it in Fairbanks, but thought it was useless. I had found them on the internet before I left Arizona. I called and talked to a nice guy who said BRING THE CAR BY when I got there. It would be a quick transaction, which I wanted.

I walked in and said I wanted to sell my car. They looked at it and made an offer.

SOLD.

Then I explained I would need it for a couple days. I asked if I could drop it off as I was heading to my plane. They said no problem and offered me a ride to the airport when I dropped it off.

Next I went to the airport. Not to the main terminal, but around back to the small plane area. There were two options to Anaktuvuk Pass, Wrights and Warbelows. My first flight would be with Wrights, and I wanted to drop off the bulk of my freight early. It was about 10 boxes. Two days later I would bring the last couple bags and the cat. And that finished the errands that needed to be done.

So now I had one more free day to kill in Fairbanks. After that I was tundra bound.

My thoughts turned to golf, the default thought in my brain.

There are 3 golf courses in Fairbanks. Two of them had just closed for the season. Like the day before I arrived. But Fairbanks Country Club was open, for one more day. I had dragged 4 clubs with me since I dropped most of them off in Kanab with my sister. For you golfers out there, I had a putter, a driver, a wedge, and a five-iron. All you need in a pinch. And Fairbanks.

I went out there in the morning, and I talked to the pro. He talked to me about where I had been, and where I was going. He liked the fact I was playing his course LAST.

This was a 9-hole course. I headed to the first tee and swung a few clubs to get warmed up. I had not played for a couple weeks. When I pulled out my driver and tried to swing it, there was a problem. Somehow, during the trip I had broken the shaft of the driver. It was broken about 5 inches down from the top. The break was within the grip. It bent like a knee joint. Right where I held the club. What would Tiger do? I adjusted my grip and played on. I had 4 clubs, and one of them was broken. MANLY GOLF. ALASKAN GOLF.

I hit my first shot. Solid, but high and a little right. I invoked a tradition going back to ancient Scotland, the Mulligan. A re-do. I only do it once, when applicable. If the next shot goes in the trees, I play from the trees. My next shot was perfect, splitting the fairway with a slight fade, which the hole demanded. As I walked down that first fairway I felt like I was in a dream. Golfing in Alaska!

I chose the 5-iron for my approach shot. The shot was solid and landed on the fringe of the green. Now skill came into play, so I had trouble. I settled for a bogey. Again on the second hole, I hit a great drive. Weird. But it was mediocre from there on. I played that 9 holes at 6 over par, with four clubs. One broken. AND I only hit my 4th club, the wedge, once.

The round was concluded after nine holes.

I looked for the pro, and asked him if he could repair my club. He said it was no problem. Turns out I would not need it for some time. I asked him if he could hold onto it until I came back through town. Once again, NO PROBLEM. He asked for no money. We exchanged phone numbers and parted. Later I would see ads on local TV where he was mentioned as a top pro in Alaska.

Next morning I went to Alaska Park And Sell and finalized the sale of my car. At least I THOUGHT I did. More about this later.

It took 10 minutes, and I was done. At that point, my worldly possessions were very few. They said they would transfer title and send me a check.

It would take a few days. Frankly, I was in no hurry. Then I loaded up a couple of bags and the cat in their car and they took me to the airport.

We pulled up to the small building which housed Wrights Airlines. The customer area was pretty small. I checked in and sat down with Fluff in her cat carrier. There was no security, no checkpoint. I was getting a taste of travel in The Bush.

A guy walked up to me and said ARE YOU JOE? I responded to the question in the affirmative. He said he was the pilot, and that we would be leaving soon, a bit early. This was because I was ready, and I was the only passenger! These are small planes that hold 9 people (or 45 cats), including the pilot. I could have ridden in the co-pilots seat, but BILL the pilot had his lunch sitting there.

So I sat in the first seat behind the co-pilot seat. When I looked around me I saw the plane was full, but not with passengers. It was packed with cartons of cigarettes and Coca-Cola. These are staples in these Alaskan villages. Fluff was stacked in her carrier on a pile of Marlboros, soon to be napping.

I chatted with Bill as we taxied to take-off position. But he put on his headphones and I shut up. The airport has two parallel runways. In general, the small planes use one runway, and the big boys use the other. Next thing I knew we were screaming down the runway and taking off. Right then I was thinking WHAT THE HELL AM I DOING HERE??!!

I love flying. Years ago I was a couple of hours away from getting my pilots license, then I moved away and discontinued the lessons. My instructor was a friend who was giving me a good deal on the cost. He charged me for the rental time of the plane, but his instruction time was free. I miss you FRED!

While flying I spend most of my flights staring out the window trying to keep track of where we are. Checking out landmarks. Looking for golf courses. I had been anticipating this flight for some time. Small plane at a lower altitude flying over The Brooks Range. I had a perfect view of the airplane instruments and knew our airspeed and elevation, all that stuff. But there was also a couple of small radar screens where I could see the various mountains we were passing through.

The first part of the hour-and-a-half flight is over rolling hills with many streams that are unique in that they do not follow a straight line in any way. They turn back and forth constantly, like a never ending snake. You can see that this years streambed is different than last years. The old bed is dry and sitting nearby. I guess the spring thaw causes a lot of runoff changes. And that thaw is sitting everywhere with countless lakes of all sizes. The color scheme is brown and green.

One major landmark was The Alaska Pipeline. We followed it north. Eventually we headed a bit northwest and lost it. I looked for the only other town on the way, Bettles.

It was obvious when we crossed The Yukon River. It is very wide and easy to distinguish.

Then the land started to rise in elevation, and FINALLY in the distance I could see some big mountains we were approaching. As we got closer I saw they stretched far to the east and west, and well north. First we passed over The Endicott Mountains. The Brooks Range was next. Bill the pilot changed course several times as we started to descend, now flying amongst the peaks. We were flying close to a couple of big mountains, passing a summit, then turning downward following the curve of the mountain. Then a big valley came into view below us, and Bill pointed to a spot far ahead in the middle of the valley and said THERE IT IS. At first it was almost hard to see, but soon the runway stood out.

For a small town with a population of 350 it has a BIG runway. EVERYTHING comes to Anaktuvuk Pass via air. And they have some big pieces of road equipment, as well as construction equipment. I heard it all came in on a C5-A Galaxy. The runway is a modern 5000 footer. There is plenty of flat ground for that runway, and it dominates the town when viewed from the air.

The town lays in a valley which is THE Anaktuvuk Pass. Maybe a mile or two wide, but many miles in length east to west. On each side are large mountains. But this pass is a huge pathway through all these mountains. And the HUGE Caribou herds in northern Alaska use the path for their migrations. In fact, Anaktuvuk Pass means PLACE OF CARIBOU DROPPINGS. No shit!

From the air, it was very obvious that I had now found the MOST REMOTE place I had ever visited. For miles and miles there was nothing but Nature.

The plane approached and I was taking film of as much as I could. The town was a cluster of a hundred buildings next to a big runway with a couple roads extending out for a couple miles. Then we were over the runway. Bill kept flying, as he only needed a bit of it to land. We touched down and pulled toward the only building right by the runway. Turns out that was the Post Office. The airport itself had no building or facilities.

We came to a stop and there were a few people waiting. The first person waiting to meet me was a local State Trooper. Did I mention Anaktuvuk Pass is DRY as far as liquor goes? You cannot even possess it. So, bootlegging is a real issue. The Troopers meet EVERY plane as it arrives, and decide who should be searched for contraband as they disembark. He looked me in the face and said HELLO. I said the same to him and went to get my stuff from the rear of the plane. I know he knew who I was, and he let me pass untouched. As they did every other time I landed.

I turned around and there was Minnie, my new assistant, and Larry the Board President. Nice greetings from all. After talking a minute I saw the rest of the staff had already loaded all my luggage and boxes onto a pickup truck. Minnie drove the truck and gave me a quick tour of town which took about five minutes. There were hardly any newer buildings, most were needing some repair. But the school was very modern, as is typical in rural Alaska. There were no paved roads.

We pulled up to my new house, which was part of my pay package. Two bedrooms, one bath. All I needed, actually. Basic furniture. It was a bit disappointing after being in a nice house back in Arizona. But I remained positive. Frankly, it was one of the nicer houses in town. Due to its unique color, I gave it the nickname THE PLUM SLUM. It really was not that bad.

And talk about a location convenient to work! The house was on an intersection of roads that formed a Y. When I crossed one of the roads, I was at my office and the Hotel / General Store. If I crossed the other road I was at the restaurant. This was all under my authority now. I was also responsible for the fuel depot down the road a bit, as well as a satellite TV operation. My title was General Manager of Nunamiut Corporation. Pronounced "NEW-nuh-mute." This was one of many Native American Corporations formed across Alaska. They are run by Board Of Directors and pay out dividends, if profitable. IF.

There is also a city government and facilities. Nunamiut ran the commercial side of things. I quickly found out that unlike most corporations, profit is not a driving factor. The real goal was to keep things running and cover the costs, with any profit considered as gravy. It was not unusual for the Corporation to give cash to someone having financial problems. Like paying for a funeral. Not very business-like.

We went inside the house and everyone was talking to me, introducing themselves and asking questions. When I looked up, all my stuff was brought inside. Everyone made sure I had all I needed, and I said yes. Eventually they all left. Fluff was happy about that. She came out, sniffed around, then hid under the bed. As usual. I tried to get unpacked and get acclimated.

I started work in the morning.

# ANAKTUVUK PASS

My first night was uneventful.

Next day I formally met my staff. I learned more about my assistant Minnie. And I talked with my new boss Larry. My office was in the same building as the General Store and the hotel. The General Store was a beehive of activity. Many of the locals who came by for something stuck their head in to say hello.

I felt welcome and needed.

As I went through the books and files, it was obvious there were problems. Many problems. For one thing, the checking account was in chaos. There was no way it would ever get balanced, I just wanted to get it close.

And I could tell it would be interesting working with the eight Board of Directors. In a town of 325, do the math. Odds are, EVERYONE in town is friends or relatives of a board member. Or both.

I jumped right in, which the board preferred. So I counted on input from my staff to point out areas to deal with. Eventually I would figure out where they were wrong. It would take time.

Almost immediately I saw they felt differently about their jobs than I did. There was no sense of duty, no sense of service. I got the impression they thought it was all owed to them. No initiative. If I did not tell them what to be doing, they killed time until I did so.

My staff was 95% Native American. There was one white guy, the chef at the restaurant.

The fuel depot was manned by Jimmie Jack. He was a solid guy, dependable. He was the exception to what I said earlier. He was a steady guy, someone I could count on. His past included a period as a helicopter pilot in the army. Now he sat in a shed a quarter mile away taking care of fuel sales to the locals. Some cars and trucks, and a lot of snow machines and quads. He also helped the weekly DC-6 unload its fuel. All fuel was flown in. 5000 gallons at a time. At the peak of the gas crunch a few years back, Alaska had the highest price of fuel. And Anaktuvuk Pass was the highest in the state, and the USA. Not always good to be #1.

The General Store / Hotel was run by Minnie my assistant. Her husband was on the Board of Directors, as well as her sister. She was a capable employee who knew everyone in town. Many of the customers who came through to get cigarettes or sodas spent time talking to her. It was good, and it was bad.

Minnie was part of a dance team that participated in Native American competitions, including The AFN Conventions held once a year. She had years of experience and knew a little of everything. But she spent a lot of time playing computer games.

There was a second lady who helped Minnie, ELFRIDA. She was considered a temp. I began to learn that TEMPS were the backbone of the company. Employees had a habit of just disappearing for no reason and with no notice. The temps filled in when needed. It was almost a full time job being a temp. Except the temps did not want that, so there were a LOT of temps who were happy to be in a long line for the next job.

Kenny was a driver who delivered fuel to the residents. He was Minnie's brother. Are you starting to get the idea here? He had absenteeism issues. He also helped to hook up satellite cable to the residents.

Then we had Tom, the head chef at the local restaurant. The only white guy on the payroll. He was smart and married a Native American girl, so he got several dividend checks due to several kids his girlfriend had. He had an assistant chef occasionally. Otherwise he had Matt, a young guy who seemed to have a good attitude as a helper. Finally there was Molly, an attractive young lady who also helped at the restaurant.

Then we had that list of temps who could fill in when needed. Like I said, the temps were a regular part of business here.

It was the type of place where someone would punch in all the others who were late. Being late was pretty bad as the longest commute in town was about 5 minutes. So there was a time clock, but there was always a question as to WHO was punching WHO'S card.

My first couple of weeks were spent getting oriented. There was work to be done in every direction I looked.

The General Store was a real mess. No merchandising, just lay the product on a shelf or the floor, and maybe someone will buy it. The area around the front counter was unorganized and messy. It was embarrassing, at least for me. The hotel was acceptable, but could use some work. Then there was a big project in the hotel / general store area that I wondered about. It was an area that seemed to be a stocking area for product or parts. A lot of shelves were built, but to hold what? Possibly snow machine parts, but I do not know. It was obvious there was a lot of work done recently, but to what goal? Nobody knew. More likely they just did not want to tell me.

My office was also a mess. Piles of paperwork that needed to be filed. There was no organization. Drawers stuffed with all sorts of junk. OH, but there was a TV with all cable channels. A first for me, at least in a work office. Later I considered it a plus when I worked over the weekend by myself and turned some sports on.

So I had to prioritize. There were issues in organization, personnel, goals, and equipment. What fire needed to be put out first? The company needed a great manager to shake things up. Well, here I was!

Number one, I can do NOTHING without a willing and able crew. I immediately questioned everyone and their motivation. But I gave them time. It was like taking over a sinking ship, and it would take time to figure out what hole to plug first. Basically, every aspect of the operations needed some work. So I stumbled through the early days of operation. I relied on staff and Larry's input as to what needed to be done, and HOW. I considered all options they gave, knowing that none of them may be correct. Looking back, I should have cracked the whip and said MY way or NO way.

Soon I figured out that this was a crew who needed to be told what to do. It was common to find everyone chatting instead of working. It was common to find people on the computer playing games. When they knew I saw them messing around, they continued unless I told them to do something else, like their JOB. They were used to having their way. There was no professionalism. But I knew I was in uncharted territory, 150 miles north of The Arctic Circle. I held off on big changes and criticism. My priority was to get the big picture straight in my head.

If the same circumstances existed in the lower 48 where I was prior, people would have been fired.

But I was patient and wanted to see what people could, or could not do. This soon was obvious.

I soon knew what my biggest obstacle would be. Unfortunately, she was supposed to be my biggest asset, Minnie. Her family was one of the founding families in Anaktuvuk Pass. There was an intersection in town of two streets. One street was named MINNIE AVE. The other street was named after her family last name. Say no more. She was well established in the town. She was friendly and knew EVERYONE. This did not mean everyone liked her.

She was even considered for my position, but did not have the education.

Minnie seemed open to my ideas at first. I am used to employees doing exactly that, following my requests. That is, good employees. A successful change in management is as much contingent on the manager as it is on the staff.

Meanwhile, just getting used to living in THE BUSH was a job for me. Everyday life in Anaktuvuk was unique.

There were a lot of vehicles, just not a lot of roads. It took two minutes to drive through town only because that stop sign slowed you down. One road went west out of town. It followed the runway and kept going. About a mile. It turned into a narrow road, then a path. At the end of it you felt like there was nobody around. The path was for snow machines heading out on the tundra. Then it was SCATTER.

I knew the other direction, east, led to THE DUMP. So it was a couple weeks before I went that way. Too bad. It was awesome!

When you leave town, it is sudden. The houses just stop, then it is you and the tundra. It is an ice road heading east. The cemetery is on the right, then wide open. You go up a gradual rise, only seeing the dump at the last minute. It is just a fenced area with an incinerator in the middle. Why the fence? Still do not know. Maybe to keep the caribou from damaging the incinerator?

Too bad, the fence ruined the view from certain angles. Basically the road ended with an awesome view of THE Anaktuvuk Pass. This was a huge path leading east to west through The Brooks Range. There were huge mountains north and south, but a broad valley about a mile wide that split right between them. The view had to be seen to be appreciated. As well as the lighting. It looked off into infinity. Nothing definitive in the distance. Just the mountains to either side. And at the time of year I saw it, WINTER, the colors were pastel and unbelievable. It was almost like looking at a painting. I took some photos, but they looked fuzzy. In fact, they were not.

I took some hikes, but it was difficult. There were no broken trails during the winter. So it was a matter of trudging through the snow in -10. The best hike I took was to the north from my house toward Blueberry Mountain. I had to climb a steep ridge right away, then climbed a long uphill slope. It offered a great view of town. After some time I reached the crest, only to see I still had a long way to go to get to the mountain. I was not prepared for that long of a hike, so I enjoyed the view and headed back.

At one point I took off my gloves for a couple minutes to take some pictures, and soon was losing feeling in my fingers. I put the heavy gloves back on, but never quite recovered. I took other hikes, but they were much shorter. Unfortunately I would not have the chance to hike when it was warmer.

Daylight was also an issue. At that time of year, there was not a lot of it. It got light around 11 AM and started to get dark again at 2 PM.

There were examples of the town being a bit rustic. There was no cell phone service. Right now this is being changed in all of the Alaskan Bush. Most houses had typical land line phones, but some did not. Some houses were very primitive. Only in the last few years did the town put in sewers and flush toilets.

The biggest difference I saw was the use of CB. Yes, same CB as in trucker convoys. It was the "phone" for many people. Everyone monitored one specific channel. Someone would say "Mary, MARY?! Go to 16." This meant Mary, if listening, would go to that channel where they could have a semi-private conversation. Of course anyone else could switch to 16 and listen in.

One day we were in The General Store where we always monitored Channel 9. Someone in town was drunk and ranting for over an hour. It was on the main channel everyone turned to. Minnie acted like this was a regular thing, and we could always turn it off if we wanted to.

There was only one grocery store in Anaktuvuk. It was a part of the corporation I managed, but for some reason, it was not under my authority. Too bad, as it would have been the first thing I would have worked on to improve. A few years ago The Board determined it would be better to separate the grocery from everything else. I think it had to do with the manager at the time, and their capabilities. It was a bad decision.

EVERYONE had to buy from the store, including me. My first impression was EMPTY SHELVES. Most of them. Then there were the high prices. Approximately twice what I paid in Arizona.

At first I got used to buying what THEY HAD, not what I wanted. Then I saw the back room. It was PACKED with food. NOT fresh produce or meat, THAT was always going to be an issue. But packed with all sorts of products that I could use. Products that everyone could use. Products not on the shelves.

The manager, who I was friends with, told me the whole story. They did not have the manpower to get the stock out. Too many people quitting, or not showing up. And nobody to hire. This was all too familiar to me in the short time I was there. THIS was the reason I knew I was in an unworkable situation. I was no miracle maker.

The whole town was a victim of their own incompetence.

As I mentioned, Anaktuvuk was dry as far as liquor goes. I got through the inspection every time with no search. But others got through, too. And they were carrying. Bootlegging. There was plenty of liquor available. Most of it was ROT GUT cheap stuff. R&R was the big one. If you wanted it, it would cost you. $250 per fifth. And it sold quickly.

The town voted it dry. I heard that they were reconsidering. FUNNY. The biggest drinkers thought it was best to remain dry. They thought it would be too big of a problem. I soon found out that most of the towns BIG WIGS were drinkers.

Anaktuvuk Pass is much the same as many other villages in The Alaskan Bush. It is totally dependent on airplanes.

EVERYONE and EVERYTHING that is in town arrived via airplane.

Anaktuvuk had 4 flights that came through on an average day. That is a lot for a town of 350. It tends to be the locals going "to town" to shop or do business. It cost $175 for a ticket. It was very typical to have flights delayed and cancelled due to weather, or lack of passengers. I took at least 2 flights where I was the only one on board. But there was a lot of freight, which made it worth it.

Everyone in town knew the flight schedules. The planes would announce their arrival with a low pass over town. That gave anyone interested a chance to meet the plane as it landed. There was also another clue the plane was near, the runway lights come on. They are activated by the pilot as he approaches. When I looked out my office window and saw the lights on, I knew a plane was landing.

There is no terminal at the airport. Just a runway.

15 minutes before the plane lands there is NOBODY at the airport. When the runway lights come on people start to show up on ATV's, snow machines, and cars and trucks. Oh yeah, the police show up too. The state troopers. They meet every plane and have the right to search for contraband (liquor) being smuggled in. I never saw anyone searched in the times I met the plane, but that was only a few of the many flights. I ended up talking with one of the troopers and found him to be a pretty nice guy just doing his job. Once I went into his office and he showed me a wall of liquor bottles, still full, which they had confiscated..

Every few weeks I had to order a plane load of fuel for the village. It carried 5000 gallons and was flown in by an old DC-6. This plane was a real show when it came in and left, and it used a good amount of that runway. It was LOUD.

So I took a couple weeks to get my feet wet, then I jumped in and did my job. Finally I realized I WAS THE BOSS. Yes, the Board had authority over me, but it was passive. I was the one who needed to make decisions and answer for them. The Board wanted that from me. We had our regular Board Meeting where I would be given direction and goals. Then I went and did the job. That is what they were paying me for. I wish I knew that from the beginning. The Board Members all had regular jobs that kept them busy.

Once a month we had a Board Meeting. I participated in it with a regular report on the ongoing business of the corporation. Larry, the President ran the meeting. It followed parliamentary procedures. Larry ran the meeting and was in control. If you wanted to speak, you asked to be recognized. Motions were made, then seconded. I found it a bit ironic we were following these strict procedures in a small town in The Alaskan Bush. It made me nervous.

The first meeting was soon after I started, less than 2 weeks. So I was under the gun to get a handle on the situation of the company, then report on it to the Board. Suddenly the day of the meeting was there. Larry called me to help out, as I had no CLUE what was expected. He had me pull out some reports from previous meetings to use as a guide. I had to prepare a minutes of the last meeting, which I did not attend. And I had to prepare an agenda for that nights meeting. I know computers fairly well, but this was a new system and I was now short on time.

Oh, then there was the honorarium. MONEY. Every board member got $150 just for attending the meeting. This explained the usual perfect attendance. The meeting was scheduled for 6 PM, and it was 5:45. I am trying to print up 8 checks on a printer that was not cooperating. Plus I was arranging to have some soft drinks and snacks available. Just as I was finishing, about 5 minutes late, Larry came in to see what was happening. He said everyone was there and WAS I READY?

I said yes. As ready as I could be. My only concern was speaking in front of people. There were only eight, and I had only met 2 of them. I grabbed all the paperwork and checks and walked with Larry to the meeting room. It was a 30 second walk down the hall of the hotel, but that was 30 valuable seconds as Larry gave me last words of advice.

I walked into the room of mostly strangers. A good ice breaker was me handing out their checks. Then we passed out the minutes, agendas. Larry took over, but right away I was asked to call roll call. I read each name from a list and asked if they were present. Hell, we all were sitting at one table. At least two names were mispronounced. Then I was done for awhile.

Of course, I had to make notes on everything that was said in order to generate minutes for the NEXT meeting. There was general discussions on some business opportunities, mainly with oil and gas developers. A tribal elder had recently passed away and the corporation was kicking in some money to help the family. Next thing I know Larry was asking for the monthly business report.

That was ME!

I introduced myself, and said I had been there for just a couple weeks. I told them I knew the checking account was in chaos. This was a bit interesting as Minnie, the cause of most of the imbalance, had been asked to attend this meeting. Normally this is a private meeting of the Board and myself, the Manager. I also told them it appeared we were having cash issues, but I had to dig into it further. There were a number of pointed questions, all from strangers. WHAT WAS I GOING TO DO? I basically told them I had no idea. (I was the fourth Manager in 2 years. One of them, Howard, put in 2 stints. He was kicked out when he dated too many younger tribe members. He was older, and dated ladies who were older than 18, but still appeared too young to everyone else.

They hired someone else who did not work out. So they hired Howard back in desperation. Now, he had recently quit. That is when I was hired.)

This was a tough position to fill. First, you probably needed someone single. There was not a lot to do for a partner. That person needed to be OK with living in a desolate and primitive location. OH YEAH, the tribe also wanted someone with a degree and experience.

Frankly, the meeting went pretty well. The whole thing was held as a big screen on the wall showed a Monday Night Football game with the sound turned off. It hit me somewhere during the meeting that I should not be nervous. These people were just looking for help. For someone who would stick around and make improvements. It was they that needed to be nervous.

The next couple meetings went very well. I felt much more confident, even though I was always giving out negative news.

My arrival in town was just before the upcoming AFN Convention. Alaskan Federation of Natives. Each year there is a convention. It lasts a week, and the site rotates between Fairbanks and Anchorage.

I heard about it when I first arrived, as it was just a couple weeks away. We talked about it at our first Board meeting. There were arrangements to be made. Who would attend? Who wanted to stay where? We ended up having to rent rooms with kitchenettes, at a much higher rate. NOBODY at the convention needed a kitchenette. They just needed a bed and a bathroom. And that was it. NOBODY was cooking. They were all using their per diem to eat well at local restaurants.

The per diem was nice, $150 per day. Seven of the eight Board Members attended. What a surprise.

I cut the checks and sent them to Fairbanks. I had the impression the whole convention was just a reason to party. Maybe not for everybody, but most. Hey, I should not judge. I would probably do the same myself.

While I am sure there are legitimate meetings that are productive, I quickly learned that it was mainly about drinking. How did I learn? Well, each day the convention went on, one of the board members called me obviously drunk. He called me at 9AM when I came to work. He had been up all night. He made it clear he was interested in keeping me around, obviously tired of the new managers constantly coming through. It always ended up with him telling me he could offer me a 30% raise. Well. He WAS the treasurer. And he was buddies with my boss. Four days in a row he kept this up. I had work to do, but he was babbling in the phone. I knew it would never happen, although I later learned that it may have been possible.

One of the senior Board members was Riley Morry. Shortly after my first Board meeting I got a call from Riley. I only remembered he had participated in the meeting as much as anyone. He seemed a bit old fashioned and stuck in his ways. But when he called he was very nice to me and supportive. He told me to not worry about all the political CRAP and just do my job. And he should know, as he held many positions over many years. This included Board President. Just another one of many.

Riley was a drinker. Near the end of the convention nobody remembered seeing him. So someone went to his room to check on him. Trouble. Riley was dead. He had been drinking. To some it was not a surprise. To all it was a sad loss.

Most of the village went to the convention, including Minnie and several of my staff. So I was on my own. Sure, with most of the village gone things were slow. But I had my hands full.

For one reason, our postal lady, the only employee at the post office, decided to go to the AFN too. She did not give her boss enough notice to get a substitute. So they just shut the whole Post Office down. Post Office closed. I had a weekly change order from the bank in

Fairbanks due. This is the cash we use to run our business. With no postal employee to accept it, the money flew back and forth between Fairbanks and Anaktuvuk. Several times. This meant that we could not cash checks, including payroll checks of the local residents.

I had personally had issues with this LADY. I think her name was LARA. When I went to get mail she would make me wait even when I was the only person there. The game was on, and I played. I said nothing. I stood there as she hand-stamped everything within range, and then re-stamped to correct her errors. We were on opposite sides of the counter, yet neither acknowledged the other. ME, I just wanted to see how long she would IGNORE a customer. SHE was doing the best she could. Sad. She would be fired anywhere else. Here she was the all-star. The only star. She was the best employee, and the worst. At the same time. She should be an X-employee.

If I pissed her off, my mail would take a lot longer. I think it was already on a general delay, both incoming and outgoing. Hard to prove. Our company got a few bills that were past due by the time we got them. Finally I called the Postmaster General. When I complained he immediately knew the postal employee in question. He admitted she had other complaints. Then he explained it was impossible to hire a replacement. He had an open job listing posted, with no takers. So they continued to use an employee who they knew was incapable. It is hard to believe the post office is ready to go belly up.

OH, just raise the price of stamps. AGAIN.

So the AFN convention ended and we expected everyone to return. Of course, the weather was an issue. Now EVERYONE goes on standby. It takes awhile for small planes to catch up. Minnie took 3 days longer to return. I was getting used to the absenteeism. It was obvious they did not care, and they were losing any respect I had for them. Hey, in a few months another manager would roll in and they would play the game again. Gee, why are the small villages dying off?

A week after the convention the community mourned Riley and a part of the past was lost.

A productive part.

Now we get to KENNY.

Kenny was the brother of my assistant Minnie. And they were both related to a couple of Board Members. A little bit too cozy for me.

The trouble started when Kenny told me he would be gone a few days to do work for his Native American Association. I do not remember the official title of this group. But I was the new guy and did not want to confront agendas unknown to me, no matter how frivolous. It appears this was an escape for Kenny to have a few (hundred) drinks in the "line of business." This info came to me from people who knew Kenny.

So I took advantage of the huge pool of temps in town. It was interesting to find a great worker as a temp. Someone who was good enough to be considered for a permanent position. But as soon as that was mentioned there was usually a negative reaction. That worker was doing a good job as he was happy knowing it was all just temporary. They did not want a real job, usually.

As a Manager, I like initiative in an employee. That is the best situation for me in my position. All this person needs is direction. Give them a priority and get out of their way. I never got this vibe in Anaktuvuk. There was an attitude of do the minimum, then have some fun until told to get back to work. It was the constant default situation.

Slowly I would realize it was a battle I could not win. But that comes later.

Kenny was supposed to be back in a couple days. It became a week. I would think a concerned employee would call if he was delayed in returning to work. But HEY, maybe that is just me.

Then after a week, he just showed up and punched in. He asked Minnie what was going on that day. I went out and asked him to come to my office so we could talk. He had no clue that he may be in trouble. Evidently he had done this before.

So we had a little chat. It ended with me telling him I had a temp for the day. I assumed he would not be in for work, just like the last few days. I told him to punch out, that we did not need him today. He acted like he was just fine with that. Obviously he was fine with it for the last few days.

But then it went HIGH SCHOOL. He left and told his SISTER Minnie what was happening. She got upset and ignored chain of command. She went right over my head and called my boss Larry. This was the moment I realized Minnie was not an assistant I needed or wanted. She went from helping me fix problems to being a problem. If they do not see me as the boss, I may as well pack up and leave.

So I just sat and waited for the inevitable phone call. The phone rang in a few minutes. I knew it was Larry. He asked what was going on and I told him.

Larry knew the politics involved, and he supported me right away.

But I went to his office and we had a talk. I told Larry this would be no good. I needed some authority, and if this was the game I had to play, I wanted to leave. WHAT authority did I have? Did my assistant have more pull than me? If so, BYE Joe. I was telling him this was my two week notice. It was not what I wanted. This was a fundamental problem that had no solution. It was very frustrating, as I was so new to the position. I remembered my conversation with Sherry in Fairbanks when she explained this would be very different from what I was used to doing.

I was totally convinced I was not going to change my mind. And I knew this was very EARLY, and I wondered if I was over-reacting. I did not like it. But I had given my notice. So I sat there and shut up. Larry started to work on me. And he hit me where it counted. He agreed with me. There had been power issues with Minnie and previous managers. I was not the only one. What a surprise. Whether it was earned or deserved, Minnie had assumed a certain degree of power. And this was bad, as she was just a senior checkout girl in reality. But this was Anaktuvuk Pass…

Larry agreed that Minnie was a problem, and he also agreed he did not know how to handle the issue. And he also said something needed to be done.

Larry reaffirmed my authority, and we were cool. I thought I would last more than a couple months. Maybe now I would, now that Larry knew where I stood.

All I know is that in anywhere but Alaska, Kenny would have been fired for missing a week. SEE YA. I had been in management for almost 30 years, but I had a lot to learn. So Kenny remained, but he was on my SHIT list. I was not worried about Kenny, he was just a driver. But now I knew I had issues with Minnie, my assistant. I knew I was on my own.

After that, I did my job and she did hers. Well, she did what she had been doing all along. Not really doing her job, if you know what I mean. And we had a different relationship now.

Early on, just after I arrived, Larry and I had some meetings where he tried to establish policy. Show Joe the ropes.

One specific item Larry brought up was payroll advances. The corporation had a policy against it. Evidently it was an issue that needed to be discussed. The problem was employees needed money before payday. When they took the job they knew payday was every two weeks. If everyone wanted their money before payday, it would be an accounting nightmare that would never end.

It happened to me the first week. And it was Minnie. She wanted money for books for her kid in school. They always have great reasons. They rarely said, I need liquor money. She put it to me as if I was the problem. YOU MEAN YOU DON'T WANT TO GIVE MY KID BOOKS FOR SCHOOL?

Have YOU ever asked for a payroll advance? Have YOU ever heard of anyone asking for pay to be paid ahead of earning it? I have not. But I now knew this was Anaktuvuk, and we had different rules.

Larry had warned me about these advances, and sure enough it happened right away. So I called Larry and told him about Minnie's request. At first he said NO, then asked what I thought. He refused, but eventually caved in. As usual. THAT is the problem. Do it once, they expect it again. Technically, they have earned their money. But it causes a lot of work and extra expense to pay on the employees terms. Personally, I would never consider asking my employer for the advance. That option would be way down the list, if at all.

Larry could have let me be the authority, the NEW guy. Looking back, I probably should have said NO and left Larry out of the loop. At this early stage I thought Larry wanted to be a part of this stuff. WRONG. Larry wanted me to take charge and make the decision. I was used to having a boss. But in this case I WAS the boss. At this point, I just did not understand that. Larry could have told Minnie it was all up to me. And then he could have told me to say NO. JOE, just say NO. And there would be no exceptions from now on. But that did not happen. We both gave in to the request and Minnie got her money.

And it continued to happen. Eventually I realized it was my decision, under my authority. I did not call Larry anymore. But employees talk, and others knew the favor was granted to Minnie. So the requests continued for the same thing. It was hard for me to be the hard ass as I was the new guy. It was obvious to me it was going to be tough to get the employees on my side. So every time an employee asked me for pay ahead of time, I gave them the standard speech, and ended up caving. Then I had to call Sherrie in Fairbanks who did payroll. SHE was the only one who had to do extra work for this FAVOR. And I heard it from her. But it was my decision. As I write I KNOW it was a bad decision.

Well, Minnie was given the speech from me and Larry before we caved, so she knew our position.

Then poor Tom, the chef at the restaurant, walked in and asked Minnie how HE could get an advance of pay. Minnie had no desire to help him.

LET THE GAMES BEGIN.

Minnie said it was against policy. So one week Minnie asked me for the advance and got it. Next week Tom asks Minnie (I wish he had come straight to me) for that same favor and she says it is against company policy. Suddenly there was a big argument between Tom and Minnie. It happened as Minnie worked the counter at the general store with customers all around. It did not matter to her. EVERYONE but me knew Minnie and what she was like.

But I was learning quickly.

So Tom comes in my office with a red face. Tom is normally a pretty mellow guy. But now he is PISSED. He explains his position. He knows others have gotten advances, and now he needs one. Plus, he has some history with Minnie. There is a feeling Minnie does not like white folk (Tom), making ME feel semi-uncomfortable in MY position.

So I said OK to Tom. He was a good employee, maybe my best. Never absent, worked hard. That put him way above the crowd. I have no problem with doing whatever I can for good employees.

Well, Minnie got word of my approval and all hell broke loose. She comes in and asks what about the policy against cash advances? I told her it was my decision, and that I agreed to do it. Just like we did for her. Why is Minnie so mad? What business is it of hers? So once again she is on the phone to Larry. This time I did not wait for Larry to call. I rode down to his office.

I am not sure anyone really understands my frustration at this point.

After the first incident, I had done a lot of thinking about this position. I knew I could do the job. But I was assuming I had a crew I could work with. AND I assumed there were the same standards here as everywhere else. This meant all employees get the same chance. A warning after any problem. Maybe two warnings. THEN, it is time to make a change.

Well, my entire crew were problems waiting to happen. OK, Jimmie Jack and Tom were pretty good. When I had the first problem with Minnie, I told Larry my boss that I felt I was stuck with her. What would it take to fire her? She was married to a board member, and she was firmly entrenched in the community. A road was named for her, another for her family. There were only a couple roads total. Larry did not answer my question. He encouraged us to learn to work together. I tried. Until she went running to daddy again.

This time I was determined to either fire Minnie, or QUIT. There was no hope for change. Who would I hire to replace her? Nobody was dropping by to fill out applications. There was nobody currently employed who I could promote. My best 2 employees were in positions that were higher than the position Minnie held, so they would be demoted. And nobody else was worth consideration.

It was suddenly very obvious. It felt like I was in a situation I could not win. The corporation had ongoing trouble holding onto managers. Their best candidate was the guy who I replaced. Howard.

Suddenly I saw the big problem. Many of the young folk were heading out of town to go to college, and never returned. The only people hanging around were the elders. This is the same problem many small villages in Alaska now have. These small towns are dying off, and I am not the miracle worker to change it all. Frankly, I think it is a logical thing. Change is constant. There are no real opportunities for young people to make a living. Unless they want to live a life of subsistence living, there is not a lot of logical reasons to stay in the village.

I gave my notice. This time I was firm.

Larry seemed stunned. I said I would stay two weeks. I knew this would cause problems, but Larry was used to them. He had a look that said HERE WE GO AGAIN. I felt bad about it. But I could not worry about them, it was time to be a little selfish. I had no job to go to. It would cost me time and money, and I had no game plan yet.

Meanwhile, just as all this other CRAP was happening, the job was getting interesting for other reasons.

And I knew I still had a job to do.

While I was having trouble with the employees, business was still happening. I could have just left, but that was not my style. I wanted to do whatever I could to make the transition smooth. Plus I had nowhere to go at that point anyway.

Ever since I started the job, I was having trouble with the checking account. There were automatic deposits made as sales were made via credit card. And there were old checks floating out there, written by Minnie while she tried to handle things in-between managers. But she neglected to note them in the check register. They were payments to vendors, and some were pretty big. When they were finally deposited in a bank, they would just bounce due to insufficient funds. This was a problem.

You want to talk PROBLEM? Lets mention the cash drawer in the general store. It is located in the same building where my office was located, as well as the hotel. They sold a little of everything. It was mainly cigarettes and soda pop. But they also sold clothes, sporting goods, and even snow machine parts. Most of it was cash business.

The store also ran transactions for the fuel depot, which was down the road a quarter mile. It was all done by radio. When a customer purchased fuel, Jimmie Jack would call our location on the radio and give the details. Name of the customer and the amount. We would then bill them, or they would drive up and pay in cash. Either way, we handled the transaction. A lot of cash went through our drawer. The hotel mainly housed contractors staying for a certain period of time to do a job. The rooms, Spartan as they were, cost $175 a night. A three week stay added up quickly.

Each day, we had to balance the drawer. There was no reason it should not be PERFECT. When I ran stores in the paint business and elsewhere, the drawer usually WAS perfect. To the penny. If the drawer was off, I had to explain WHY to my supervisors. If it was off a couple times, I could expect an audit. Someone was either stealing, or they could not add or subtract. Either reason was a problem.

So imagine my surprise when I was told by Sherrie in our first meeting that the drawer was almost ALWAYS off. BIG TIME. It was often off by hundreds of dollars, sometimes over a thousand. Right from the beginning I suspected Minnie. She always mentioned she needed more money. There seemed to be no concern as she handed me a closing report where we were $1400 dollars short. I expected a slightly different reaction. Of course, I was just the latest manager. So I analyzed the system and tried to fix it. Maybe the system was fine, and we had a THIEF. Or maybe we had a bad system as well as a thief.

I have learned there are 2 conditions which promote theft. They are NEED, and OPPORTUNITY. These conditions were both present.

My biggest problem with Minnie was she was the wife of a Board Member. And related to another Board Member. And firmly entrenched in the community as a member of one of the families that formed the village. Not her, but her relatives. GOOD ENOUGH. I would have to photo Minnie pulling cash from the drawer to have any hope in proving her guilt to family and friends. I had no proof, just a lot of suspicion.

I realized this was a huge issue for me, and always would be until it was corrected.

Meanwhile there were other BIG RED FLAGS. That check book. I assumed nobody had a clue as to balancing it. That certainly appeared to be the case. Or was it someone with a bit of brains just stealing? Maybe it was both. There were too many things happening at once, money floating in the system, where it was impossible to truly balance that checkbook. We had a stretch where we bounced a few checks. It was embarrassing and frustrating. We were always cutting it close with minimal cash funds. The situation was ripe for writing bad checks without knowing it.

I had learned Larry, Board President, always had a secret way to get cash. Suddenly $100,000 would show up. Some endowment to the Native organization. Native businesses lead an interesting manner of business. It is not like the business I was used to. You know, where we had to earn profits.

Money had been tight all along, well before I arrived. I looked back at the old transactions in the check register, and noticed several big deposits that were put in the account. Then everything was fine, and the corporation was good for a few months. But things always ended up in trouble again. It was not very clear to me where the money came from. Larry made a few phone calls and it suddenly was there. I was not there long enough to figure out the cash source. I am sure it was legitimate, and I know it was a mystery.

Living in Anaktuvuk Pass was a learning experience.

In the short time I lived there I realized the local folk did not need a lot of money to live. Maybe that is why they gave their job and working a lower priority. They got a lot of their food from hunting . Subsistence living. And they lived in inexpensive housing. Add to all of that they are given a decent amount of money just for being born in the village.

DIVIDENDS.

# DIVIDENDS AND FINANCES
# IN THE BUSH

First off, the Native Americans get shares in Nunamiut Corporation, but that rarely is a source of dividend income. Then there is the Permanent Fund. This applies to ALL Alaskans who have lived in the state for at least a year. Finally, there is Arctic Slope Regional Corporation. This is the money maker, although that has not always been the case. But the last few years have been very good to the shareholders. A nice check is cut when there is a profit. It can happen twice a year. The big one is in the Fall. Then, in the Spring, any change left over after the dust has settled from the previous year is given out as a $2^{nd}$ dividend. The Fall Dividend handed out while I was General Manager was a record high dividend. Every shareholder gets 100 shares to start. GIVEN when born. The Fall Dividend in 2007 was $42.21 per share. That is $4221 for the typical shareholder. For EVERY member in the household. That goes a long way in The Bush.

Don't get me started (OOPS, too late) about the benefit to everyone in handing out these dividends. Up front this appears to be a noble gesture. Certainly the money is needed and benefits many. But it appeared to me, a casual observer who probably knows nothing, that too many people are COUNTING on this dividend. The dividend is not guaranteed, but over the last few years it has been a regular payday.

It seems to me that this discourages looking for other sources of income. Like a job. Nothing beats a hand out.

I may have mentioned somewhere along the line that Nunamiut offered a check-cashing service at our General Store. We cashed all checks from small to big. There was no bank in town. There was not even an ATM. We had a monopoly. And, we charged NOTHING for the service. It is the best deal in the U.S. I was stunned when I heard this, especially since the corporation was having cash flow issues. The corporation evidently felt the same as me and was instituting a service charge just as I came on board. BUT, it was way up in the air as being in stone. Larry called me shortly after I was in my position and told me to notify everyone in town about the new policy. The new policy voted in by The Board. By the time I had the signs printed up, he called back and said not to do it. He felt too many villagers would be upset. I still do not know if that came from him or The Board.

The point here is that we cashed checks. The Corporation had to maintain a lot of green cash to handle this. We usually had 30 to 70 grand in the safe. Each week I ordered 30 to 70 grand MORE from the bank. We cashed a lot of checks and deposited them regularly. Lots of money being passed around. We were BUSY, just not making any profit. But that is another story.

As I was ready to leave the position, Permanent Fund Dividend checks would soon be mailed out. AND, in a couple weeks there was a much bigger challenge coming. The ASRC Dividends.

In both cases we would be cashing a LOT of checks.

We would need about $750,000 in cash for the Permanent Fund checks. And we would need almost 1.2 million in green for the ASRC dividends. As I said, the corporation was not exactly swimming in cash. If we had 1.2 million in the bank account, we would just make a withdrawal and take care of it.

Then Larry made a suggestion. He explained that the previous year the corporation was able to borrow up to $200,000 to help with cashing the checks. Since the checks were deposited right back into our account, the loan was able to be paid back in just a week or two. The bank allowed up to $200,000 at a time. The corporation paid it off then did it all over again. And again, if needed.

Larry seemed to feel that the role of the corporation was more of a service organization for the community. The goal was to cover expenses and everything after that was gravy. Nothing about making a fair profit. He KNEW that fat check would show up. It kinda takes the urgency out of things. Just like with my employees. They knew they could risk losing their jobs and not show up, over and over. Because 2 or 3 times a year, the fat check would show up. It would all work itself out. Why work for money when it would show up sooner or later? Until then, caribou every night.

Larry asked me to talk to the bank about another loan. We did business with Key Bank, the same bank who loaned us the money last year. I gave them a call. Sure, they sounded very positive about another loan. Then they started asking for crazy stuff like financial statements and accounting books. We had these things, but if they were to determine whether we got a loan or not, we had a problem. The documents were not very positive.

Dave Case, the company lawyer in Anchorage, was involved in this whole process also. He pointed out to me that Nunamuit had cashed in a large financial asset within the last year to (Surprise!) help with cash flow issues. This was a problem NOW because that was the main collateral Key Bank used to grant us last year's loan. It was now gone.

Dave had been talking to another bank about a short term loan to get us the cash we needed. Darned if that bank wanted the same financial info that I had been asked to provide with KEY BANK. Just because we wanted a couple hundred grand! Dave told them he would get back to them, then he e-mailed me and said it was not going to work. He did not even tell that bank we had no good collateral. Frankly, this loan would have been pretty much risk-free. We would use the cash to cash ASRC checks. Then deposit the checks back into the bank. ASRC is well known in Alaska, and their checks are as good as gold. The bank had to know that.

Meanwhile, Larry was doing his own thing. He had conversations with ASRC about giving us a short-term low interest loan to help cash THEIR checks. While they were not a bank, they were open to the idea. Larry forwarded me several e-mails to keep me in the loop, but it was just a lot of fluff not going anywhere. However, Larry personally felt encouraged. He told me to follow up with ASRC and he gave me the name of a lady to contact. Then he took off to Barrow for a roundtable meeting involving many North Slope villages.

With all 3 of us working different angles, it all came to a head. At this point, 1 was still working Key Bank. Dave Case had JUST run into trouble with his bank, NSB. Larry had a good feeling with ASRC. After he put it in my lap I began to put 1 and 1 (and 1) together. It still added up to nothing. Dave also had punted to me, saying to keep trying with Key Bank and ASRC.

I talked to the ASRC lady who had been told to GET THIS DONE by ASRC President Bobbi Quintavell. The lady was in New Jersey on other business, but she told me to talk to banks we worked with and use the ASRC name to get things done. ASRC did business with many banks, and they had a lot of cash. Hopefully this clout would help us, once we provided our financials. Oops.

Dave Case and I had both run into the same roadblock. We were unable to provide solid financial statements. So Dave and I talked. We figured to just deal with it on our own. The residents were just going have to deal with us running out of money. Otherwise they could open a real bank account for direct deposit, or fly to Fairbanks to cash a check and get drunk. It actually sounded like a good plan for the long run. If you live in the Bush, you give up a lot of conveniences, like a bank. Everyone would be able to cash their check, just not right away.

About 2 hours after Dave and I had that conversation, I get a call from
Larry. He was now in Barrow for his meeting, and Bobbi Quintavell
happened to drop by. They talked and they called me via conference
call. Larry explained he had figured a way to get us money, not knowing
Dave Case AND myself had just failed. Now I am talking to Bobbi
Quintavell herself, and she is telling me to call a certain bank who really
wants business with ASRC. They will do whatever it takes. She tells me
to call NSB Bank, the same bank Dave Case has been talking to for 3
weeks. I gave the guy a call, just for a joke. I felt that maybe ASRC was
NOW putting pressure on NSB to get this thing DONE. I assumed
(!!) that ASRC knew we had been talking to NSB already WRONG.
When I contacted Mr. NSB, I told him where we stood. I was now
putting it all together. Time to be blunt. I asked him if he was going
to need the same financial requirements everyone else needed. He said
yes. So that was that.

We were all back to square one. The corporation would have to take
care of the issue itself, and that is the way it should have been all along.
Nunamiut never was a bank, we just cashed checks. Besides, another
dividend would show up in a few months and we would go through the
whole mess again. Time to get used to it.

The Permanent Fund came upon me quickly and I was not really
prepared. Nobody explained to me what to expect. I ordered a large
cash order from the bank to be prepared, $75,000 or so. But it only got
things started. First, I did not realize the dollars needed to satisfy this
demand. Maybe $400,000. Second, there was the frenzy of the masses.
ALL the checks showed up at one time. They all came in on one plane
and hit the Post Office at the same time. Anaktuvuk Pass has the worst
Post Office in the US, but I digress. Around 11 AM that day, there was a
stampede to the General Store. Suddenly our sleepy store had 40 people
waving $1500 checks at us. With more on the way. We cashed as many
as we could. When we got down to a few thousand left, about NOON,
we made the announcement to come back later. OUT OF CASH.

I called Sherrie in Fairbanks and she came to the rescue. Literally.
She went to the bank and made a big withdrawal. The bank was very

hesitant in giving Sherrie all that cash. They knew her and trusted her, but she was a single female picking up a lot of money. About $90,000 in green. Sherri ended up getting her husband Wayne to escort her. The bank was reluctant, but allowed it. Thanks to Wayne! He had his own job with the Alaska Pipeline, but helped us out. Sherri caught the 7:30 AM flight and was up in Anaktuvuk by 9:30. I gave her a bottle of water and she stayed right there with the plane. I handed her all the checks from the previous day so she could personally deposit them when she returned to Fairbanks. She would be back there by 1:00 or so, and would go straight to the bank. This sped up the turnaround time quite a bit.

Normally our deposit went out on the plane every morning. The plane flew 350 miles to Fairbanks. For some reason it took 5 to 6 days to clear at the bank. I even called the Postmaster about it. I felt the Post Office in Anaktuvuk SAT on it for a day or two. Part of the issue was the package was insured and had to go through secure transportation. This in itself added time.

Everyone in town knew when Sherri arrived that morning with the cash.

When the money was coming in, Minnie made a general announcement to the village over the CB radio. ATTENTION! THE CORPORATION WILL HAVE MORE CASH AT 10 AM TO CASH YOUR CHECKS. The word spread like wildfire.

I took the 30-second drive back to the store with the cash. Everyone was waiting in line. Minnie ran the only cash register, and I counted out the cash. She cashed the check, then I took their receipt and gave them what they were due. $90,000 lasted about an hour and a half. Then we were out again.

At that point I made a decision.

It was about time for me to be leaving Anaktuvuk Pass. My notice was served and I did my time. But it was a bad time to leave with all of this dividend CRAP going on. Plus, I saw a chance to have some fun while helping out the company. Where was I going to go? I had no job waiting for me. I saw a few trips to Fairbanks over the next several days. Get out of town for a day or two at a time. Fly over the Brooks Range. Stay in a nice hotel, eat some decent food. Return and repeat it all again. Someone had to do it. Besides, Sherri had her own job to do.

I called Sherri and we came up with a game plan. I would catch the 9:30 AM Wrights flight to Fairbanks and Sherri would meet me. We would drive over to the bank, get the new cash, and return to the airport for the 1:00 flight back. I had about an hour to do this, but it was do-able. The problem was the plane was about a half hour late picking me up in the morning, so the window became very small to catch the return flight. I knew Sherri and I knew she could deal with it. When I took off it was the pilot, me, and one other guy.

As I flew over the awesome tundra, Sherri was scrambling in Fairbanks. It should be said here that while all planes have a set schedule, it all becomes just a piece of paper with numbers on it the day it happens. Anyone involved in taking or meeting a flight from or to the Bush ALWAYS calls the airline to get the current status. It all changes very quickly. I knew Sherri would hear my flight was late. I KNEW she would get the cash herself. She was a smart lady.

When I landed, I called Sherri. No answer. I had a short conversation with the lady at the counter telling her what I was up against. She said I had no time to leave and come back. The plane took off in about a half-hour. Then, the airline desk told me I had a call. It was Sherri! She had the cash and was in the parking lot with SANDWICHES. She knew there was no time for me to eat otherwise. A GOOD LADY! I went outside and there she was. She had $90,000 in cash and a sandwich I could never finish. DAMN SUBWAY. Can't they make a simple sandwich with a couple ingredients?

We ate our lunch in the parking lot, well, half of it. Then we said GOODBYE. I gave her a large deposit of checks to take to the bank, she gave me the cash. I went back into the airline office and the same lady

I talked to earlier expressed surprise. She said she did not know I was flying back, because I had not checked in. I had the conversation with her earlier and told her I was returning on the 1:00 flight. I guess that when I went to the parking lot I voided all that. So she went upstairs. Probably to talk to the pilot who thought he was done for the day. She came back and said I was OK. I figured out soon enough why they were hesitant. I was the only person on the flight. The pilot comes down, introduces himself, and we go out to the plane.

I had been the solo passenger before this, and THAT pilot gave me the safety speech. This guy said nothing, maybe he was pissed. And when he moved some of his stuff around before the flight, I SWEAR I saw an empty beer bottle. That is why they call it Warbelow's Air Adventures. Soon we were taxiing to the runway and taking off.

I sat way in the back and felt like I was in my own air limo.

It was clear, mainly, but there were some distant grey clouds. No sun. I took some photos on the way and enjoyed the flight. We got near Bettles and I noticed a change in the flight. We circled over town to gain altitude, which was unusual. Shortly after that we entered the gray zone. There was no sense of motion while looking out the window. Everything was gray as we flew through the clouds. This was the tone for almost an hour. I finished the last half of my Subway sandwich. As I watched the pilot I knew he was making some flight adjustments. We made a few turns instead of doing the straight line route, and I just kept waiting. In my mind I was wondering if we could land. I had not seen any land for an hour or so. I knew we may have a problem and was OK with turning around, but the pilot indicated nothing to me.

After awhile we were going down, obviously getting ready to land. The clouds broke open and I could see the ground. There were TREES. Fir trees. This was not Anaktuvuk. No trees in Anaktuvuk, only tundra. We came in making a sharp turn over a river and dropped down to a runway. In a blizzard. I was guessing where we were at. Bettles? WRONG. It was Allakaket. Already on the way back to Fairbanks. We touched down and then the pilot said AS YOU MAY HAVE

NOTICED, WE ARE NOT IN ANAKTUVUK. He explained he flew over Anaktuvuk and could see nothing, so he decided to turn around. Hey, all I knew was we were going back to Fairbanks where there was a nice room, food, and whiskey waiting for me.

When we pulled up to the airport in Allakaket there were 6 passengers waiting. We were only stopping for about 10 minutes. However, by the time they all boarded the pilot had to go outside and clear the snow off the wings. He climbed out on the wings and swept off the snow with a broom. It was coming down pretty good. Big wet flakes.

We took off and headed back to Fairbanks, a little over an hour away. It was in the dark and I saw only a couple lights until we got to the metro area. I recognized a pumping station along the Alaskan Pipeline on the way. It was very cold when we approached Fairbanks, and it was an unworldly view. There were columns of smoke or steam rising in the air from various locations. They rose high in the night sky. When they hit a different layer of weather high up they spread out. So it looked like the city had a few mushroom clouds rising over it as we were landing.

When we touched down, I had to do some scrambling. Call a cab, then go to the Westmark Hotel where I had no reservation. The cab driver made a stop for me to get a pint of whiskey. My first drink in over 2 months. Just before I got out I remembered I had no cash for the liquor. OH, except for the $90,000. I broke the seal on the bank bag and took out a short term loan. Then it was off to the hotel.

Nice place, nice room. I looked at the cash in the bag and saw it had all become unbundled. A lot of the bills were loose. I took it all out to organize it. Threw it out on the bed. It was a lot of cash in one place, and I ended up taking some photos of it. When I got settled in, I called my sister Sue in Santa Fe, New Mexico. Told her the latest of my Alaska adventures. Then I hit the dining room for a nice meal. They were putting up Christmas decorations and it was the week of Thanksgiving. I joked about that with the decorators. Over the next couple weeks they learned to recognize me.

At 7 AM next day I was at the airport and on the early flight back, this time on Wrights Air. It was dark most of the way, getting light only as I neared Anaktuvuk. I still caught glimpses of awesome scenery in The Brooks Range. When I landed, most of the town was waiting. They had called the airline and figured out where I was with the money. After I got settled in Minnie told me they had heard my flight go over the town the night before, but could not see it. They were surprised it did not land, especially when two other late planes DID land shortly after. The opinion in town was Wrights would get you there if possible, but Warbelows would turn around if it was borderline. Hey, there were BIG mountains all around. If the pilot doesn't feel good about it, he headed back! This was life in The Bush.

Everyone who really needed cash quick seemed to be satisfied at this point. They cashed their checks. The line dwindled. I ordered more cash from the bank and we got over that hump.

But the ASRC checks were coming soon. They would be the BIGGER project.

Soon after I gave my two week notice to Larry, Dave the lawyer pointed out to me I had agreed in my contract to give a 4 week notice. It was somewhere in the fine print. Fine. Knowing I was soon leaving made dealing with Minnie much easier. I talked with her only when I had to. At the time, I was set to leave Thanksgiving weekend. However, I decided to stay a while longer to handle the ASRC dividends. I ended up staying seven weeks. Besides, the Holidays was not going to be the best time to look for a new job. I did not want to leave Nunamiut in the middle of chaos. Last but not least, SOMEONE was going to have to take a few trips to Fairbanks to turn checks into cash quickly. I will never get tired of flying over Alaska, especially the Brooks Range. Nice hotel, good food. I would stay until the check cashing was done. Plus, I continued to make some money.

The job turned from being a chore to having a little fun. It was good for me as well as THEM.

The ASRC checks were being mailed out on a Friday, December 7th. Nobody was sure when they would arrive. I had to assume Monday. Knowing Alaskan mail service, it could be anytime that week.

Making plans was almost impossible. The plan was simple, much like when we got the Permanent Fund checks. Cash the checks until we ran out of cash. Catch the next flight to Fairbanks. Then I would deposit the checks, wait for them to clear, withdraw cash and go back to Anaktuvuk Pass. Repeat it all again until everyone was happy.

It was hard to figure how long the process would take. EVERYONE did not need to cash that check right away. Some waited until they flew to Fairbanks themselves. Others did have direct deposit. Normally catching a plane at the last second was not a problem, seats were usually plentiful. There were 4 flights in and out of town each day: Two in the morning and two later in the afternoon. EXCEPT, now that money was coming in to town, a lot of people would use the cash to fly to Fairbanks to Christmas shop or get drunk, or both.

Planes fill up quickly when there are only 9 seats. I started guessing and reserved a seat here and there, but it usually did not work out. I had to be flexible and do what I could.

The whole town was waiting for the mail plane on Monday. It came, but did not have any checks. I had a reservation for the afternoon flight, so I cancelled. Tuesday looked pretty strong. Sure enough, the checks showed up. By the time the people started coming in to cash them it was 11 AM. In a matter of minutes there were 50 people in line. The first person handed us a check for $6200 to be cashed. We had about $75,000 in green cash to use, it would not last long. A lot of people in line were not going to get their money that day.

Minnie rang up the transaction. I stood there with a box of money off to the side and counted out all the cash. Everyone was patient while they waited in line, knowing they were soon to be holding THOUSANDS in cash. Everyone knew each other, it was a party. Even when I told the people in line we would soon be out of cash, most remained there.

The corporation had a lunch hour from 1:00 until 2:00. When 1:00 approached, we still had plenty of cash. I looked at Minnie like she MAY think about working a while longer. Yeah. She read my mind and loudly announced she was going to lunch at 1:00. There were 20 people in line, and nobody complained. They would have done the same thing. My goal was to take a pile of checks for deposit and catch the 3:30 Warbelows flight. Hey, when in Anaktuvuk, go with the flow. The slow flow. So I went to lunch.

At 2:00 everyone returned, the line reformed. By 2:30 we were out of cash. I grabbed my bag of checks and went to the airport. Soon I was over the Endicott Mountains and Brooks Range. An hour and a half later, we landed in Fairbanks. I had a little business just down the road at Wrights airlines. When I got there they were just closing up but helped me out. Then I called a cab.

When it arrived 15 minutes later I was the only person around, waiting in the parking lot. I saw the cab coming and stepped out to the middle of the parking lot. There were only a couple of street lights on, and lighting was minimal. I should mention here that Fairbanks had about 8 inches of snow in the last couple days, and was about -20 at the time. I was getting cold and was glad to see the cab arrive. It was so dark I thought they may miss the parking lot, but no problem. A young lady was driving, CHERYL. When she pulled in she was sliding all over in the parking lot. The first thing she did when we left was a full DO-NUT in the parking lot. On purpose, just for the fun of it. She had no idea who I was. Got my attention. But we had fun. She told me how she had to bail-out in a ditch earlier in the day when she was coming up too fast on some stopped vehicles. If I were her, I would probably not mention this to a rider. Maybe the liquor was loosening her lips. I had her stop for a whiskey run, and she slid up to the parking spot. Almost like she was testing me. When we came to any red light, she locked up the brakes and skidded to a stop. But we got to the Westmark Hotel with no major injuries. I still have her card.

I called Sherri about picking me up for the morning bank run. As usual, she was up to the task.

Next morning she met me after I had a quick breakfast. We made the deposit and pushed the bank folk about a quick turnaround on availability of funds. These were ASRC checks, everyone knew they were rock solid GOLD. They told me the best they could do was a 24 hour turnaround. OK, Sherri dropped me off at the hotel. I now had most of the day to take care of some personal business.

Three months earlier I had "SOLD" my car at The Alaska Park and Sell. They had messed around getting the title and final payout. I really did not care, as they were giving me just about what was owed on the car. The Park and Sell was having trouble and was soon to go out of business. I did not know for sure, but they had STILL not finalized the sale of my car. When I heard this, and I knew I was leaving, I called and said I WANT IT BACK. I was waiting for a hassle, but they were very good about it. I got a few months of free storage out of the deal. There had been a problem with an employee embezzling, and the whole operation was shutting down. Kathi, who I met when I dropped the car off, was the owners daughter. She became my contact. Nice lady! I set up several appointments to meet her, and kept changing at the last minute. She was very patient. Finally we would meet today for me to get my car back.

It was a ten minute walk from the hotel to the Park and Sell. Kathi was a little late and I was starting to get a bit cold waiting for her, but she showed up. I was concerned my car would not start after not running for three months. Sitting there in the cold of FAIRBANKS. When I got there I saw it was parked in their GARAGE! I turned the key and it fired right up. Kathi pulled out some paperwork and said some repairs had been done on it. I thought HERE WE GO. But it was minimal and reasonable, like an oil change. She asked if I could pay about $100 in total. I had about $63 in cash, and she could not run a credit card at that point. I gave her what I had and she said FINE.

I had more to do. First, get insurance for the car. Second, I needed plates. I did not notice until after I left that PARK and SELL had removed my Arizona plates. All I had were Park and Sell advertisement plates. Third, I needed to pick up my golf club which I left with Tom at Fairbanks Country Club three months earlier. I had all day. My deadline was to be back at the bank tomorrow at 9AM and make a withdrawal. Then I had to kill a little more time, since the first plane I could catch was at 1:00.

So I made a couple phone calls, and thought about running my errands. Since I had about 3 hours to kill in the morning, I decided to blow it all off for awhile. I called Sherri and suggested lunch at Big Daddy's BBQ. Same place we went when we first met. She was game and soon we were eating pulled pork sandwiches.

Next morning it was a cozy -10 when I woke up. Had a quick breakfast, then met Sherri in front of the hotel. I felt uncomfortable driving with NO PLATES. We hit the bank and I left with $130,000 in green, a new experience. She took me back to the hotel and dropped me off. I checked out and went out to take care of business.

Obviously, my first priority was to get my repaired driver. My dad gave me this club a couple years back. He was visiting me in Arizona and just gave it to me. It was completely unexpected. At the time I had gone through a spell of BAD golf. On the other hand, HE had resurrected his game on the strength of his new driver. My dad has always been a good golfer. He was the reason I got interested in golf at a very young age. He took me to Rawiga Golf Course in Rittman, Ohio where I played along with him using only a putter. Almost 50 years later I NOW hit a putter from off the green as soon as it makes sense. I have done it from 70 yards away. My ROOTS.

When he gave me this driver, I was stunned. I knew he loved the club because he had told me all about it. It had been a big help to him, but he gave it away. Frankly, it DID turn my game around. I could step up and swing hard and I was confident where the ball would go. I still do not know why he did it. He lives on a nice course in Louisville, Kentucky. He plays most of the year. When I pushed him he said he would get another driver he wanted. I love my dad! He did buy a different driver and still usually kicks my ass. He is almost 90 years old!

When I tried his new driver, I liked it even better. My dad is a smart guy.

I went to Play It Again Sports where Tom worked during the off season. The day before I saw a TV commercial for the place and it mentioned Tom by name. Famous. When I went in he was there and was very helpful in giving me info about the best courses to play in Alaska, especially south where I was headed. I paid my bill and was out of there in 15 minutes.

Next, insurance for the car. Took another 20 minutes. I figured I even had enough time to hit the local Dennys for breakfast. It is the MOST NORTHERN DENNYS in the world, as the sign says when you drive up. When I walked in there were about 30 soldiers from the nearby Air Force base, Eielson AFB, paying their INDIVIDUAL bills. When I left in about a half hour they were just finishing up. It was about 10:15, I had to be at the airport at Noon.

Time to get my plates, which was on the way to the airport. I had no idea what I would need to do at the DMV to regain the ability to drive, but I had a certain amount of time to do it. I could finish WHATEVER on my next trip back in a day or two.

When I went into The Dept. Of Motor Vehicle office, I was stunned. The place was almost empty. The lady at the counter said it was slow even for Fairbanks. I told her I wanted plates. She said I needed an emissions inspection, plus I also needed to get my pink slip since I just paid for my car in full. Not a problem. While I waited for that I could get temporary plates. The lady told me there was a place across the road where I could get my emissions test. I drove right over and was done in fifteen minutes. Then I took that back to the DMV where I had to wait five minutes in line. Another five minutes later and I was leaving with temporary plates. The whole process took less than an hour. I even had a chance to buy a fast food sandwich to take with me on the flight.

I made the seven minute drive to the airport and parked across from the airline. This time it was Warbelows. There is a self-pay system to park there. You fill out a form right there and drop it in the slot, which is not real convenient when it is MINUS 10. I got there a few minutes early and checked in. I sat for about twenty minutes, then Dottie at the counter called me over. She said there was a problem. There was bad weather north and they were going to have to cancel. This was fairly common in the Bush. However, I had a job to do and had to try all options. There was a flight scheduled to leave in a half hour at Wrights, about a third of a mile down the road. It would not take much time to see if that flight was still going. As I said earlier, I had heard from the locals that Wrights would get you there if Warbelows was on the bubble.

After I just paid for four days parking, I got in my car and drove to the WRIGHTS parking lot. I ran in to see if they were flying. They looked at me like I was nuts. HELL YES they were flying. Maybe Warbelows had only me on the flight and cancelled, but that did not stop them in the past. When I asked them later, they said if one person was booked, they would fly. Maybe they got a different weather report.

So I ran out and paid AGAIN for a few days parking. When I went back to the small terminal there were many people from Anaktuvuk Pass flying back. I had gotten the final seat. Several people looked at the paper bag I was carrying and asked IS THAT WHAT I THINK IT IS? I made no comment. Ripe for a robbery.

We left on time and once again there was a large line when I arrived at Anaktuvuk. But, it was not quite as bad as the last time.

I spent that night in my own house, and flew out again the next afternoon. I felt this was probably the last flight for cash. More people than we expected had combined Christmas shopping with cashing their check in Fairbanks. As a matter of fact, the plane was packed when we flew out on the afternoon Warbelows flight. Before I left I had a conversation with Larry, the boss. I told him this was probably the last run for cash. He suggested we have one more Board Meeting when I returned. That was the last thing I wanted. He pushed for it, and I said NO. At this point I had nothing to lose, or gain. I told him I had no idea where I was spending the holidays. Christmas was now just four days away. I now had to take care of JOE business. After awhile he backed off, because he had to. He even mentioned that he would be in Anchorage over the holidays and we should get together for some drinks. I told him MAYBE, but it was a long shot.

It was -20 in Fairbanks when we landed. Fairbanks is often one of the coldest spots in the state, usually colder than Anaktuvuk Pass and even Prudhoe Bay in the far north. I had a medium jacket and not too much else. While I did have gloves, they were more suited to twenty above, not twenty below. And I had to walk the one-third mile to where my car was parked at Wrights Air. It was dark and very few cars driving by. I started walking fast, then broke into a jog. It is amazing how quickly the cold takes effect. By the time I got to my car I was hurting. I was barely able to get the door open as my fingers were frozen. THANK GOD the engine turned over. It sure hesitated, but she kicked in. I sat there for about 10 minutes and still could not feel the heater. I started the drive to the hotel hoping that would help. By the time I felt some warmth, I was there.

Every car in Fairbanks has extra heaters in the engine to keep the engine warm when the car is parked in extreme cold. A plug hangs out the grill up front. Most parking lots in town have plug receptacles where you can plug right in. The heaters keep the oil from FREEZING. A jumpstart at this point only makes it worse. Every car has these heaters, except MINE. I just came from 120 degree Arizona. I needed to make it through another week or so and everything would be better. My plans were to head south to Anchorage. It still got cold in Anchorage, but hardly ever -20.

I had the routine down by now. Checked into the room, went for a good dinner, came back and got a good nights rest. Made the deposit, and had to kill a day. Picked up the withdrawal cash next morning then caught the 1:00 back to Anaktuvuk. I was pretty sure this would be the final trip, especially when nobody was waiting at the store for me to arrive. I had gone from ELVIS to DOOFUS. Minnie made an announcement over the village CB system, but few people cared.

It was over.

And it was then I knew it was time for me to leave. While I did not know how many trips I would make, I was surprised it was all done after three round trips. Of course, one of those was double.

It was 10:30 AM. Just getting light. There was no crowd waiting at the airport. When I walked in the general store there was no line. Only a few people showed up to cash their check. I left to pack up all my stuff. I also cleaned up the place. That night I got a call from Larry. He asked me what he could do to get me to stay. He was willing to give me a 25% raise. It was interesting to hear, but I realized I would still be frustrated, just with more cash. I thanked him for the opportunity, and he thanked me. He went through this before, and he would go through it again. I slept good that night. I was catching a 10:30 flight with Warbelows next morning.

When I woke up I went to the office and gave Minnie my keys. She was glad to see me go. I was glad to be leaving her. We were both very happy. Still, the cartwheels seemed a bit much. Several people stopped by to say goodbye. Most of the village knew I was leaving, just not NOW. I told Merrilou, the new girl, as much as I could in the short time left.

Later, after I left, I heard they gave Merrilou an offer to handle most of my job, until a better candidate could be found. The idea here was she was a Native. Local. She knew the way things worked, and hopefully would be able to handle things for awhile.

She quit in a couple weeks.

Joe, the airline local contact, came by to help me get my stuff to the plane. We talked for quite awhile. When we looked outside, the runway lights were on. That meant the plane was on final approach. OOPS. Thank God I travel light. We had not even started loading my stuff. I ran across the road to my house, and Joe pulled up in a pickup truck. It was a bit ironic that we got some help from Kenny, the guy who started the whole run of problems a couple months ago. He was probably glad to see me leave too. And again, I was glad to be leaving him. EVERYONE WAS HAPPY!!

We loaded the dozen or so packages, including Fluff, and headed to the airport. It was still dark.

The state trooper was there as usual, and he told me goodbye. It was very cold, maybe 25 below zero, and windy. As I talked to the trooper, Kenny loaded my stuff on the plane. There were only a few other passengers, including a young mother and her baby. The pilot did a roll call of all passengers, as usual. He mentioned we would make a stop in Bettles on the way to Fairbanks. We would pick up a passenger and some freight. I rode shotgun in the co-pilots seat. The girl and her baby were right behind me.

# LEAVING ANAKTUVUK PASS

I knew this was a big moment for me, just like when I pulled out of Goodyear, Arizona. So I tried to soak it all in. We taxied to the far end of the runway. It was still dark. We U-turned and gunned it.

Then we were gone. Down the runway and OUTTA THERE. We banked right and I got a good last look at the town, a cluster of lights in a bleak wilderness. Then we climbed quickly to clear The Endicott Mountains. The sun peeked above the horizon and I enjoyed the views of The Brooks Range while we flew toward Bettles, 45 minutes south.

It got colder as we headed south. This was not unusual. Sure enough, as we approached Bettles the pilot told me it was -40. We made the usual low pass over the airport and town to announce our arrival. As we touched down I was thinking it even LOOKED cold.

We pulled up to the airport building and stopped. The pilot turned off the engines. Then he said I JUST HOPE THEY RESTART. Kinda surprised me. He left the plane while we had to sit and wait as the passenger boarded and some freight was loaded. I watched as the pilot did something I had not yet seen. He opened a storage compartment and pulled out some tarps. They were shaped to fit over the engines. An engine COZY. We would only be on the ground for twenty minutes, but he was concerned about the coldness. If the plane did not re-start, it was every man, and baby, and cat for himself.

So the freight was loaded. Through the large OPEN door in the back of the plane. It got real cold real quick. NOBODY was dressed for -40. Not me, not the baby, not Fluff. Sure, we all had heavy clothes and coats. But that does not cut it. I was concerned for the baby and Fluff, and I was getting VERY cold. We had nowhere to go. The pilot finally came back after removing the COZIES. And he says, WELL HERE GOES. The engines slowly turned over and kicked to life. Finally some good news.

Then the bad news.

He could not get the heater to work. Welcome to THE BUSH. None of the typical I'LL HAVE THE CHICKEN here. More like, GIVE ME HEAT. He fumbled a few minutes. And it was obvious he was as cold as us. Finally he announced we would take off, and the heat should eventually kick on. We all looked at each other. I could not see Fluff. When we took off I could not see through the windshield which had iced up. Neither could the pilot. He was looking out the side window, watching the edge of the runway. Oh, and we took off right into the sun, which was even more blinding. We banked toward Fairbanks, over an hour south. I remember admiring the view of the landscape through my side window.

But I am not lying, I could not feel my feet.

About 20 minutes later the pilot yelled the heater was now working, but it was another 10 minutes before we had a clue of THAT. Finally it got a bit warm, probably more like 38 degrees. Then we were delayed in landing in Fairbanks, as an emergency medical flight was directed in front of us. We took the long way in and finally landed.

My adventure was only beginning.

It was -50 in Fairbanks. I waited until all of my stuff was unloaded, then I took Fluff inside. I left it all in a big pile in the passenger area, and I put Fluff behind the counter so someone was watching her. There were a couple babies back there too. Evidently this was a typical duty for airline counter employees in the BUSH. Babysitting and cat sitting.

I went across the road to get my car. The car with no plug. In -50. It had been there for about 30 hours. I turned the key and hear UNG, and that was it. Jumping is not the answer. The oil is FROZEN, and it would only damage the car. There is only one solution, tow it to somewhere warmer inside and let it thaw.

I made some calls. It took a few. I guess I was not the only one having trouble with their car that day. The guy said he would meet me there in twenty minutes, and he was right on time. He had explained to me he could help me, but he was taking a car on his flatbed to another customer nearby. And I could ride along.

He knew which car was mine, and he would return.

I left all my stuff at the airport in their freight warehouse. Fluff and I took a ride in the truck as we headed to the other side of the airport. We were in a big truck that drags a vehicle up on the flatbed with a winch. He was looking for another dead vehicle for someone else. FINALLY we found it. I waited inside as he winched it up and on the bed. Then he took it to an auto shop and dumped it off. This was on the way to my hotel, The Westmark. Finally he dropped us off. Later he would return to my car and winch it up. He would take it to North Pole and put it inside somewhere overnight to let it thaw. I also asked him to install an engine heater, so I could have a plug for the future. LOVE the plug.

He would bring the car to the hotel next day.

My plan was to head eight hours south to Anchorage where I would set up camp and look for a job. It was the biggest city around with the best odds. Frankly, Fairbanks did not really appeal to me as a possible home. It saw some nice summers, occasionally seeing 90 degrees. But every winter saw a week or three of -60. And the scenery was just OK as far as Alaska goes. I should note that Fairbanks did offer views of the Northern Lights. Unfortunately for me, I never saw these. First of all, they are normally seen very late at night. And, more importantly, they require a clear night.

It was a 7 or 8 hour ride south, probably through bad weather. And there was very little in between Fairbanks and Anchorage. There was only about 4 hours of daylight at that time of year, and I was not crazy about night driving. So I would leave at first light, or just before. And then drive as far as possible until it got dark, then look for a hotel.

Next day I was waiting for my car. The guy was busy and got delayed. By the time he arrived it was 2 PM. The day was blown. He pulled up with my car on the truck bed. It was running. He dropped it and handed me a bill, which was very reasonable. He really had helped me out. I needed to get my stuff which was still at the airport, so I was going to follow him as he was heading toward the airport. We shook hands, and I followed him, simply as a coincidence.

It was still very cold, around -40. The roads were icy here and there. They could not thaw, and salt does not work well when its that cold. The truck and I headed west on Airport Way, a major city road with heavy traffic. I was in the left lane and was flying along at 35, the speed limit. A light ahead turned red. A few cars changed lanes, and I hit the brakes. Nothing. It was black ice and I was not stopping. I let off the brakes and went into the right lane where I had a bit more room. Again, I was running out of room, so I braked again. Nothing. Disaster in slow motion. When I ran out of all room and was coming up to a stopped car, I eased into the emergency lane as it was an emergency. Now I got some traction, but I slid a bit right into a wall of snow formed by a recent snow plow. I went into it just enough to get stuck. I did not even think I was stuck, until I tried to back out.

Of course, nobody stopped. I watched my buddy in the truck drive on, and figured he was gone too. For some reason, I saw him turn right about a half mile away. It appeared he was heading back toward me on a frontage road. When he went by he did not make eye contact. I figured he did not know it was me, or was not going to help. But in a minute he pulled up alongside me. COOL. He got ahead of me and attached that winch, then dragged me out with no problem. I was very thankful, and he said NO PROBLEM. That guy saved my day.

I drove the next couple of miles to the airport at 3 MPH.

I pulled up to a door at the air freight building. When I walked in nobody looked at me. Just a couple of people walking around. So I loaded everything up by myself. Walked right in, saw my stuff, grabbed a cart and loaded it up. I could have been anyone. Taking anyone's stuff. Not exactly TIGHT security. Back to the hotel where, for the first time in my life, I plugged in my car. That was a GOOD thing.

I slept very well, my last night in Northern Alaska.

It was still dark when I left Fairbanks. About 9:45 AM.

I had gotten up and had a light breakfast at the hotel. Mainly a cup of coffee. Before I hit the restaurant, I went out to start my car. After all, it was -40. But I was now plugged in with my new engine heater. It started right up. I let it run while I had my 10 minute breakfast.

When I came out for good, the exhaust was spewing high into the Fairbanks calm sky, merging with many others. I noticed that when it got extremely cold, below -20, even the wind stayed inside. It was usually calm.

So I took Fluff the Traveling Cat out to the car, and headed west. Airport Road. In one minute I was passing the spot I ran into the snow wall the day before. Not as much traffic today. But I was taking no chances. I would take as long as needed and hit the first hotel when it all got old. The estimates of driving time to Anchorage varied from 6 to 7 hours. I was in no hurry. As a matter of fact, I wanted to enjoy the ride. It was the day before Christmas Eve. Christmas eve eve.

I knew the road was slick. So I probably drove TOO slow. After I passed the airport it was all virgin road, my favorite type of road. I headed west / southwest toward Nenana about 100 miles away. The first part of the drive seemed to be the slickest, and I was still a bit gun shy from the incident the day before.

I headed into some hills and there were many curves. On one curve I felt I was sliding, so I slowed down more.

When the sun came up, it was awesome. Fire red over the mountains. I stopped for photos with my basic camera. At Nenana I crossed The Tanana River. This is the site where the ICE CLASSIC is held every winter. If you do not know what I am talking about, that is too bad. The Nenana Ice Classic. You guess in a lottery when that river ice breaks free in the Spring. Big money.

I headed south. There was a brief period of sunlight.

As I neared Healy, the clouds were moving in. When I approached the entrance to Denali National Park it was blowing snow across the road. I never got a glimpse of Mount McKinley, AKA DENALI, but I could tell there was something big off to the right. The storm was coming from that direction. And I saw some decent foothills.

I also saw the Alaskan Railroad tracks, which I followed most of the remainder of the trip. The scenery hit a peak near Denali, from what I could see. It was average for Alaska after that. As I approached Anchorage it was getting dark. I had an hour or so until I was downtown, but civilization was now apparent. I saw a couple of sled dog teams cross the road ahead of me.

Dusk had fallen as I entered Wasilla, home of Sarah Palin. Just when the drive was getting a bit LONG, I saw a sign for the Best Western at Lake Lucille. I was done. So I parked and went in to register. Nice young lady registered me. Then I went out to get my things and smuggle my cat in. One door, leading past the front desk.

So I put Fluff in a duffel bag and carried her in. She was pretty cool in the bag, mellow and quiet. I carried her to my second floor room and settled in. Then I went down to the restaurant for a nice dinner. At that point I noticed we were right on the lake, just because I saw lights in the distance across a big VOID. I also noticed the restaurant was pretty empty. Later I learned this long-time hotel was about to close. The room was nice, the food good. The scenery, which I saw in the morning, was very nice. Not sure why it closed. Possibly due to lost revenue from cat fees?

Next morning I had a breakfast at the still empty restaurant. I had also scoped out a back exit that allowed me to carry the duffel cat out without passing the desk. Next thing I knew I was on a four lane city highway about a half hour from ANCHORAGE. When I left the greater Wasilla metropolis the scenery got pretty nice. Mountains appeared in the distance, obviously near Anchorage. The Chugach Range.

A huge milestone was crossing The Knik River. Mountains, water, wilderness. All right there. Then I was hitting stop lights and I was in Anchorage. The Parks Highway fed right into downtown. Suddenly I was in heavy traffic. I wanted to find a hotel where I could stay a few days. From there I would look for a long term rental to stay as I looked for work. I cruised through town for about 45 minutes, checking things out. In 45 minutes you can see a LOT of Anchorage. One consideration was where I could take Fluff in easily. It was too much a hassle to find a place that was OK with pets. As usual I just snuck her in, and left the place with no sign a cat had been there.

Well, I chose a rare high rise hotel in downtown, The Inlet. Figured I would like a view. Turns out they were OK with the cat. So we settled into our 8th floor room. Decent. Although the view was nothing more than some nearby buildings and a street below. Soon after I settled in I heard an argument in the room next door. It was pretty loud. I knew the hotel was not very full when I talked to the lady as I registered. It was Christmas in Anchorage. So I talked to the front desk and they let me move down the hall. I got something to eat at a place next to the hotel, then I called my little sister in Kanab, Utah. I did not know that the hotel placed a premium on long distance calls (RIP OFF). So my half hour call cost about 50 bucks. I did not realize it until I checked out.

Of course, I did not have to pay it myself. An interesting perk of working in the Alaskan Bush is the exit policies of most companies. They all usually pay for the move to Alaska. AND, when you eventually leave, they pay your way home. There is no written rules I am aware of, it may be a law or not. But they usually pay the way to where you came from. I could have had my way paid back to Arizona. But this chapter was not over, and I was going to give Alaska a chance. So I asked for expenses to Anchorage.

I had a conversation with Sherri the bookkeeper. She agreed it was reasonable to pay my way to Anchorage and a few days more of expenses. It would be cheaper than going to Arizona. And until a new manager was hired, she was the one cutting the checks.

COOL.

She ended up quitting shortly I left out of frustration.

I had trouble sleeping that night at The Inlet. The nearby elevator made unusual noises when it operated. Easy to hear, and I am a light sleeper. So I decided to make a change. I needed to find somewhere comfortable for a few days. So I checked out next day after making some calls. Cheap LOCAL CALLS. I found a decent rate at The Comfort Inn on Ship Creek, right downtown near the water. They had a computer to use and a great restaurant next door, The Bridge. Nice room. Had to smuggle in the cat, but there were back doors. Perfect. I checked in on Christmas Eve. There was no Holiday Spirit. More like Holiday Survival.

When I woke up there was a foot of snow on my car that was not there last night. As a matter of fact, there was NO snow on the ground when I arrived in town. And it was still snowing pretty hard.

Merry Christmas. I watched some football and called the family. Then I got hungry. The motel had no restaurant, and the restaurant next door was closed for the holiday. I talked with the front desk and they said only one place was open on Christmas, a local diner on C Street. I checked it out. The roads were unplowed but driven on, and they were pretty bad. Two tire marks down two lanes. When I pulled in the diner was packed. Most of the parking area was unplowed and deep snow. I found a corner and got in there.

The place was hopping. I had the most expensive thing on the menu, and it was less than 20 bucks. The service was good, the food OK. Nothing special, but acceptable. I took the long way back, learning my way around town. When I got back I hit the yellow pages and classified ads in the paper. I needed to find a cheaper place to live. Something month to month so I could look for work. I saw an ad from a local realtor who had a place to rent. I called him as well as several others. It was Christmas Day, not the best day to shop around.

Next day I met him to see the place. It was in The Woronzof Tower on the corner of Spenard and Fireweed. An old section of Anchorage. This was a seven story building with condos of permanent residents. A few were now available for rent, although the regulars frowned on the rentals. ESPECIALLY on the shorter term, month to month that I wanted.

The place was nice. It was furnished and had all the needed supplies. Move in ready. And they were OK with a cat. It was secure. The only entrance was via elevator, and you needed a key. The price was a bit high, about $1500 per month. But that was half of the cost if I stayed at The Comfort Inn. I took it.

I moved in the day before New Years Eve. It would be my home for the next several months. My parking space had an electrical outlet to plug in my car heater.

One BIG selling point was the view. It was on the fourth floor, looking south. Straight ahead and to the left were The Chugach Mountains. Awesome. Straight ahead were the distant mountains along Turnagain Arm, a branch of The Cook Inlet. I had a constant show of big airplanes taking off from the airport. Many of them freight planes leaving for Asia. Many good sunsets.

Oh yeah, I looked down on the most famous bar in Alaska. Chilkoot Charlies. It is a big bar with several different sections. They feature many NAME bands who play in town, and they also have various promotional events that attract many locals. The reputation of the bar goes well beyond the borders of Alaska. It stayed open until 3 AM. At that time there was always a rush of activity. Cars and cabs taking everyone away. There were the occasional fights. I was usually asleep at that magical hour, but often awoke to see the pilgrimage outward.

One night the local police got someone they really wanted and nailed him just below my window. Many police cars. I filmed it with my old camera. There was also a shooting at a nearby apartment complex. I walked over to be a gawker. Generally, it was a nice neighborhood, but there was a negative element for a family living there.

I ended up staying there 3 months. During this time I started posting pictures on the internet, as well as starting a blog. I used a weather site on the internet as a base, Weather Underground, and I used the name of Joealaska. If you google that name you will find the photos.

So I started looking for a job.

I wanted to stay in Alaska, but it really limited my opportunities. Again I used CareerBuilder and kept the parameters wide open. While I was not desperate, I was open to anything. I was willing to hang in there until I found something decent. But there was a feeling of urgency. $1500 rent per month will do that.

My days were pretty typical. I did not do much except go through many online ads and respond. At night I kept notes of what I was doing for my potential book. I did a lot of writing regarding my trip from Arizona to Alaska. THIS BOOK!

It was my goal to get out and take a walk everyday. I usually did it late at night. Sometimes in a blizzard. ESPECIALLY in a blizzard. That winter was a near-record for snowfall in Anchorage. It missed out by an inch or two. When I arrived the blizzard started, and just continued.

While I concentrated on applying to jobs, I did get out a few times to see the area. Twice, in March, I went to nearby Palmer and played golf on a little 9-hole course called FISH HOOK. The first time it was still EARLY for golf. The course had patches of snow and ice here and there. Wet, melting ice. Slick ice. I was walking across such a patch and took a nice fall. I tried to catch myself and cut my hand on sharp ice. Bled like a stuck pig. Afterward I took some photos of the mess and played on.

Driving and walking around Anchorage, I had the chance to stumble on a moose a few times. Not literally. These huge animals roam the city freely. They are found everywhere, including right downtown. And on major highways. One day I saw one on the south side of town and I was able to stop and get close for a couple photos. For a moose it was average-sized, but still BIG. Evidently if you piss them off they try to trample you with their hooves. We never reached that point.

Another time as I was walking close to my condo, I saw a big one sitting in some bushes. If I did not happen to look to my side, I may have walked right past. It was only about 20 feet away.

One local moose gained some notoriety when he got entangled in some Christmas lights downtown. He walked around with a string of them hanging from his antlers. He stood near a downtown tavern, and appeared a bit wobbly. He was seen eating ripe crabapples, and the theory is he got a bit drunk as the fruit was fermenting. He got the nickname BUZZWINKLE. A few months later he was discovered injured and dying in a downtown alley and had to be put down.

There was some awesome scenery to explore, but I was unwilling to spend money and time doing so. Eventually it seemed inevitable I was soon to be hired, with several opportunities arising. So I took the chance to take a ride. I headed south on The Seward Highway. Driving along the water of Turnagain Arm, part of the Cook Inlet. Just the highway and Alaska Railroad tracks by waters edge, and cliffs on the other side. Eventually the road went inland toward Turnagain Pass. The area featured several landslides that winter that had fatalities. I noticed

MANY landslides that had happened within view of the road. Very close to the road.

Driving over the pass meant driving through a canyon formed by snowplows plowing deep snow. A wall of snow on each side of the road. A narrow high ridge of snow remained in the median untouched.

I drove 125 miles and ended up in Seward. While I was in town, I drove along the bay where a tsunami had hit during the big earthquake in 1964 on Good Friday. There were signs warning me of the possible dangers. I have seen some awesome film of the bay receding after the earthquake, sucked out to sea. Just before it returned as a tsunami.

I had lunch and headed back. Now it was snowing, then snowing hard. It was hard to see the scenery, and was the worst going back over Turnagain pass. The road became covered with blowing snow, but I made it back with no real problems. When I was in Anchorage, I looked behind me and saw a wall of clouds where I had been, but it was fine in town. Unfortunately, this was my only real road trip in the three months I was in Anchorage.

Several job opportunities came up. The first was Operations Manager at a local Wonder Bread plant. It was less than a block from where I was living. I could smell the place whenever I went outside, or opened my windows. I interviewed and it seemed I was in line to take the position, but they must have found someone better.

During the interview they told me they were having problems with errors in production. I had noticed a few dumpsters of bad bread outside. They told me that was a production error. Missing ingredients. After the position was filled, I noticed the dumpsters kept being filled with bad bread. Throwing out a lot of DOUGH. I could have done that job, too bad for them.

Next there was a position running a plant manufacturing mobile homes to be shipped north to Prudhoe Bay. I was familiar with these homes and had management experience, but it ended up falling through.

The biggest disappointment was with Tidal Wave Books in Anchorage. The biggest book store in town. The job required management and merchandising experience, my personal strengths. Again, it was less than a mile from where I was staying at the time. I went and interviewed with the couple who owned the place. It went very well, and they said the same. It seemed to be a done deal. But afterward someone with a lot more experience, specifically in book store management, applied and was hired.

I got a very nice email from the owner who explained they were going to hire me but found someone even better. OK. Frankly, I liked Anchorage, but wanted something a bit more unique.

It was a big disappointment. Again, I knew I would be the right choice. In the end, it was good it did not happen.

I continued to use Careerbuilder.com. In January, I had noticed a position in Dutch Harbor. My qualifications were perfect. Management background, willing to move to remote Alaska. I thought about applying, but thought NO. Simply based on what had just happened in Anaktuvuk Pass. I assumed it would be working for Native Americans again. Let me make this clear. I had no problems with Natives in general. But I found a specific situation in Anaktuvuk Pass where the work ethic was less than what I required as a manager. I did not want any chance of the same situation happening again. The people themselves were very friendly and hospitable.

As I debated whether to apply or not, the listing disappeared in a couple days. I assumed it was filled and I moved on. But a couple months later it reappeared. At that point I was getting impatient and my money was starting to dry up. I had reached the point of applying to positions in the lower 48. I even said I would move back at my own expense. I had some real interest in Idaho managing a Manufactured Home Center. I had the experience they wanted, but I wanted nothing to do with it except it would make some money.

I also had a good shot as Business Manager for the City of Ketchikan, Alaska. It is a small city in the SE part of our state, in the peninsula. I truly thought I was getting in above my head. But it was a beautiful city on the water, port to many cruise ships heading north and south through the Inward Passage. What the hell.

The nice lady who I sent the application to called me and set up a time for a phone interview. I knew I had nothing to lose, as I continued to get interest with my other resumes I sent out. It was only a matter of time. So I did the interview, and I was blunt with the answers.

When I knew the answer, I expanded on it as I emphasized my management background. If I did not know it, I laughed and said I DO NOT KNOW. These questions were usually specific to Business Manager situations in a city the size of Ketchikan. If I knew the answer to any of these questions I would have been hired on the spot. Still, I was right in the running. At the time I was getting interest from Dutch Harbor. I leaned toward the job I could do best. Not government. I told Ketchikan I had another situation. They were not prepared to make an offer NOW, but she asked me to call later if I still was interested. I had the same offer from Idaho. This all helped with my confidence.

I talked to the current manager in Dutch, and it all sounded good.

After one last conversation with my future boss, it was a done deal. I got the same package as I had in Anaktuvuk. Same salary, free housing, free vehicle. But there were a lot more roads to drive. Instead of five miles of roads, I had over twenty!

I was hired without ever having a face to face interview. Again.

Welcome to Alaska.

# MOVING TO DUTCH HARBOR

So I had my job offer, but there were loose ends to take care of.

I gave my notice to my landlord. It was a real estate agent who was a little old lady who sounded like a little old guy due to years of smoking. There was a $1500 deposit I wanted back.

My new boss wanted me to get to Dutch Harbor ASAP. I made flight arrangements for the cat and myself. The cat was not easy. Thank God I still had the papers needed for entering Canada, and YES I was still bitter.

Then I had to sell my car. FOR REAL. I went to a couple dealers, not a lot of interest. One salesman said he may buy it himself, but I doubted that. So I called the Anchorage office of Alaska Park & Sell. The same place that folded in Fairbanks. They said to bring it by.

I waited until the last minute, until I needed my car no more. Two days before I flew out, I drove to the car lot. It all took fifteen minutes. They drove it around the block, then we went inside to finalize. I walked out with a nice check in a few minutes. Then they gave me a ride back to the condo.

The day before, while I still had a car, I took all my worldly possessions to the freight hangar at the airport. I set them up to be shipped to Dutch via the freight forwarding company I was now going to run in Dutch. It was a brand new operation at the time. Now it thrives.

Next day I took a cab out to the airport. A ten minute drive. Now the big issue was Fluff the cat. I had been told that this particular plane had no room under the seats, so she would have to go via cat carrier in the cargo hold. This flight did not go too high, so oxygen was not an issue.

When I got to the ticket counter, I asked them if there was any way the cat could stay in the passenger area with me. OH NO. That would be against regulations. They told me to hand the cat to the gate attendant. OK.

These are smallish planes, 33 passengers. You board them from the tarmac, walking out to the plane. Someone near the plane will stop you and take any large carry-on bag, as the overheads on this plane will not hold it. A piece of luggage that may be a carry-on with any larger plane would now be put in the cargo hold. This is much the same as with many smaller commuter planes.

So I carried Fluff out in the cat carrier. I was a bit pissed at the ticket agent, but I knew there were RULES. I approached the plane and handed the cat carrier to the cargo guy.

NOW THE GOOD STUFF.

The stewardess was standing in the doorway up the ramp, and she saw me. When she saw me hand a cat over to baggage boy, she yelled out. NO, JUST BRING HIM ON BOARD. After all the hassle at the gate, a stewardess was taking charge.

Turns out there was room for MANY cats. There were only three passengers. Somehow I guess they did not know this at the ticket counter. The stewardess told me to just put the carrier on the next seat. Pretty obvious and common sense. Maybe not for all. As usual, Fluff slept most of the way.

We were over water a lot, but out of my left side window, which I recommend, I saw a couple of volcano cones. That is how ALL the Aleution Islands formed.

After 3 hours we descended. I saw several islands, then a road along the beach. Then there were buildings. The plane was jumping around with the wind. We leapt onto the runway, and I was home.

The end of THE ROAD.

I called the guy I was replacing, who was supposed to pick me up. He did not know I was there already. After awhile he picked me up. It was all a blur. First we went to the warehouse. On the way he pointed out the Horizon vessel that brought our weekly replenishment stock. At the warehouse the guys were busy unloading the container vans with forklifts. The place was a beehive of activity.

I met everyone very briefly. Then I was given a tour of town. Right away I noticed all the eagles. At one point we drove out on the dock at Unisea. We passed by perched eagles just a few feet away and they just stared back. The town is pretty small, but I lost my bearings right away. There are two islands closely situated with irregular shapes. Amaknak Island is where our warehouse sat, and it was much smaller compared to the main island, Unalaska Island. We also went out along Captains Bay and saw Crowley Dock as well as the bigger dock at OSI.

Then we went to my apartment. It was a bit of a disappointment. I knew it would not be perfect. The place was more like a bunkhouse. Still, it was OK. It reminded me of my place in Anaktuvuk. The Coast Guard had a block of apartments in the building. There were also apartments for the observers who came through town and went out on the fishing boats.

The apartment was actually pretty big. But the carpet was old with some nice stains here and there. The appliances were ALL old. The vinyl flooring had stains. It was 2 bed, one bath. The main room was huge. The front of the building looked out on The Bering Sea, but I was in the back. I looked at a rock cliff. Fairly often I heard rocks falling off the cliff. The good news was the fact eagles rested on the cliff, often very close nearby.

There was no furniture except a bed and a chair, and I had brought no furniture myself. I had negotiated they at least get me a bed and a chair. After that, I would add stuff as time passed. The bed was there, with new bedding. Later I saw it was a used mattress with a big stain. Then there was that chair. It looked like it was comfortable early in its life, but now it had a lean to it. Pretty significant. It was a bad first impression. Looking at the one lonely leaning chair sitting in that big living room made me have second thoughts right away. When I quietly complained about having no TV, my boss kicked in $750 and I bought one locally. Here in Dutch, that bought me a 12 inch screen that also had a DVD player. And I still use it as my only TV. My laptop and my iMac both have bigger screens.

A week after I was in town I was ordering a new mattress at my expense shipped up from Seattle.

It was a semi-rough start, but it was still an opportunity I wanted to pursue.

Now, over five years later, I am glad I stayed.

There have been adventures to describe. Big weather to experience, along with volcanoes, earthquakes, foxes, and eagles.

I have posted over 6000 photos on WeatherUnderground.com. as "joealaska."

This is probably not the end of THE ROAD. But who knows? All I know is that in these economic times we are living in, I am very happy to have this position.

At the same time, it is a very stressful job which is hard to ever really get away from. We sell food to the larger fishing vessels. These boats never sleep. There is always a crew working on them. So they can call us at any time of day. Our office phone is forwarded to me 24 hours a day, 7 days a week. It may not ring at 3 AM very much, although it has. But we also deliver at any hour. So I may get a call at 3 PM about making a delivery later that night a 3 AM.

It can get CRAZY busy on weekends. We get our weekly container vessel that brings in our food and freight for all these boats. There are usually boats waiting for us to unload and deliver to them. Plus, I have to order food for the entire warehouse over the weekend.

When people tell me HAVE A NICE WEEKEND, I think RIGHT!

Describing life in Dutch Harbor would take another book. At least.

Stay tuned. That book is now writing itself.

It will have to wait until I leave the island. That is inevitable, after what I have been through here. Every day is an adventure, but there is never really any rest. At least during the two big fishing seasons. After five years I think it could be affecting my health. I do not want my last image being the ceiling of a med-evac flight to Anchorage.

There is no doubt that Dutch is a beautiful place to work, all year round. The job is exciting and interesting. But I can only take so much. Something else is out there for me to experience.

And now the phone is ringing.

GOTTA GO!